The
SACRED THEORY
of the EARTH

edited by

THOMAS FRICK

North Atlantic Books
Berkeley, California

The Sacred Theory of the Earth
edited by Thomas Frick

Copyright © 1986 by Richard Grossinger

Copyrights of individual pieces to their respective authors

ISBN 0-938190-62-8 (paperback)
ISBN 0-938190-63-6 (cloth)

Publisher's Address:
North Atlantic Books
2320 Blake Street
Berkeley, California 94704

Cover Art: Photograph of Mani Stone and mountains in Nepal by Barbara Martz
Cover and Book Design by Paula Morrison
Typeset in Paladium by Classic Typography, Ukiah, California

Contributing editor: Richard Grossinger

This is issue #36 in the Io series and volume I of the "Sacred Theory
of the Earth" two-volume set; volume II is entitled "Planetary Mysteries:
Megaliths, Glaciers, The Face on Mars, and Aboriginal Dreamtime."

This project is partially supported by a grant from the
National Endowment for the Arts, a Federal agency.

The Sacred Theory of the Earth is sponsored by the Society for the Study of Native
Arts and Sciences, a nonprofit educational corporation whose goals are to develop
an ecological and crosscultural perspective linking various scientific, social, and artistic
fields; to nurture a holistic view of arts, sciences, humanities, and healing; and to
publish and distribute literature on the relationship of mind, body, and nature.

Library of Congress Cataloguing in Publication Data

Main entry under title:

The Sacred theory of the earth.

(Io ; no. 36)
1. Anthologies. I. Frick, Thomas. II. Series:
Io ; no. 36.
PN6014.S22 1986   808   86-693
ISBN 0-938190-63-6
ISBN 0-938190-62-8 (pbk.)

Acknowledgements

I would like to thank all contributors — not only for their contributions, but also for their enthusiasm, their interest, criticisms, their suggestions and further references, and also, in several cases, for their old and new friendships, which have been important.

For encouragement of this project in other ways, as various as people are, I would like also to thank: Andra Birkerts, Lynn Focht, Rick Wester, Jéròme Festy, Lois Frick, Don Wellman, Allen A. Dutton, Polly Scarvalone, Susan Sontag, Michelle Ebersohl, Willard Frick, Thomas Sheehan, J.G. Ballard, Flora Farmer, Howerton Lucas, Patrick McCord, Larry Mermelstein, Stephen Mitchell, Sandy Primm, D.S. Carne-Ross, Madeleine L'Engle, and The Elementals.

Contents

Introduction

A desert island in the morning, and a big city at night.
—Gabriel Garcia Márquez

Assembling an anthology is like consulting an oracle. One casts forth a topic then takes a reading, at a certain moment in time, of what the situation is "out there." Scouts report the terrain. Of course, as Walter Benjamin said, "The work is the death mask of its conception." What had I envisioned? Something perhaps more abstractly (or academically) concerned with the geomantic traditions. What has arrived is something unexpected, but much better.

The problem is: where to put the church? When the territory is new, we first learn to read the world, and then we blaze the trail. Ever after, in following and elaborating the trail, we are interpreting the text. Once the trail is there, it is difficult to go by any other route. We lose the ability to see the world afresh. Oracles, of one kind and another, are everywhere established by those who have been through before.

Geomancy, the interpretive science that lies in the background of this anthology, is divisible into telluric and divinatory branches. Forms of earth-divination exist, in various stages of decomposition, in all cultures. A true taxonomy is difficult, since everything can be interpreted, and forms of divination shade off into each other. The *I Ching* can, in a sense, be seen as a geomantic oracle. Many games (hopscotch and certain board games, for example) are devolved forms of earth-divination.

The telluric branch is less concerned with predictive powers, and more with individual vision, with teaching, with practice. One must simply learn to *see* what the earth, as a living being, has to say. Insofar as the traditions have come down to us, this branch was most strongly developed in China, and in Britain. It is this kind of material which comprises the present anthology—far-ranging individual expressions of the telluric spirit; what the earth has to say to us, from the heights and the depths, about our condition here.

Some historical and contextual material we have tried to provide through an assemblage of quotations. The consultation of oracles can still be useful, primarily in learning of the kind of hidden and forgotten material we need to make conscious again. It is time to become individually aware of the things we formerly had to be told in groups, and reminded of regularly.

But every enlightenment proceeds by virtue of a blinding vision that, though illuminating all in a certain direction, also casts profound shadows, precisely in the areas not visible from that particular vantage point. It might now well be time to return to a geocentric cosmology, yet with new awareness of the difficulties and responsibilities of such a viewpoint. What is imperative is that, as individuals, we become more conscious of the uniqueness of our metaphysical "position," in time and in space, and of the infoldedness of our consciousness, however individual, with that which gives rise to it.

We are concerned with integrating local vision and cosmic location, without falling into the somnolence of imagining that our limited conception of the "whole earth" constitutes a new "enlightenment." Theodor Adorno's inversion of Hegel — "The whole is the false" — should serve as a reminder until "garlands adorn the tended paths of paradise."

Thomas Frick
Strasbourg, June 1985

The
Sacred Theory
of the
EARTH.

Extracts

Plato
from The Phaedo

There are many wonderful regions in the earth, and the earth itself is neither in nature nor in size such as geographers suppose it to be — so someone has assured me.

How can you say that, Socrates? said Simmias. I myself have heard a great many theories about the earth, but not this belief of yours. I should very much like to hear it.

Why, really, Simmias, I don't think that it calls for the skill of a Glaucus to explain what my belief is, but to prove that it is true seems to me to be too difficult even for a Glaucus. In the first place I should probably be unable to do it, and in the second, even if I knew how, it seems to me, Simmias, that my life is too short for a long explanation. However, there is no reason why I should not tell you what I believe about the appearance of the earth and regions in it.

Well, said Simmias, even that will do.

This is what I believe, then, said Socrates. In the first place, if the earth is spherical and in the middle of the heavens, it needs neither air nor any other such force to keep it from falling; the uniformity of the heavens and the equilibrium of the earth itself are sufficient to support it. Any body in equilibrium, if it is set in the middle of a uniform medium, will have no tendency to sink or rise in any direction more than another, and having equal impulses will remain suspended. This is the first article of my belief.

And quite right too, said Simmias.

Next, said Socrates, I believe that it is vast in size, and that we who dwell between the river Phasis and the Pillars of Hercules inhabit only a minute portion of it — we live round the sea like ants or frogs round a pond — and there are many other peoples inhabiting similar regions. There are many hollow places all round the earth, places of every shape and size, into which the water and mist and air have collected. But the earth itself is as pure as the starry heaven in which it lies, and which is called aether by most of our authorities. The water, mist, and air are the dregs of this aether, and they are continually draining into the hollow places in the earth. We do not realize that we are living in its hollows, but assume that we are living on the earth's surface. Imagine someone living in the depths of the sea. He might think that he was living on the surface, and seeing the sun and the other heavenly bodies through the water; he might think that the sea was the sky. He might be so sluggish and feeble that he had never reached the top of the sea, never emerged and raised his head from the sea into this world of ours, and seen for himself—or even heard from someone who had seen it—how much purer and more beautiful it really is than the one in which his people lives. Now we are in just the same position. Although we live in a hollow of the earth, we assume that we are living on the surface, and we call the air heaven, as though it were the heaven through which the stars move. And this point too is the same, that we are too feeble and sluggish to make our way out to the upper limit of the air. If someone could reach to the summit, or put on wings and fly aloft, when he put up his head he would see the world above, just as fishes see our world when they put up their heads out of the sea. And if his nature were able to bear the sight, he would recognize that that is the true heaven and the true light and the true earth. For this earth and its stones and all the regions in which we live are marred and corroded, just as in the sea everything is corroded by the brine, and there is no vegetation worth mentioning, and scarcely any degree of perfect formation, but only caverns and sand and measureless mud, and tracts of slime wherever there is earth as well, and nothing is in the least worthy to be judged beautiful by our standards. But the things above excel those of our world to a degree far greater still. If this is the right moment for an imaginative description, Simmias, it will be worth your while to hear what it is really like upon the earth which lies beneath the heavens.

Yes, indeed, Socrates, said Simmias, it would be a great pleasure to us, at any rate, to hear this description.

Well, my dear boy, said Socrates, the real earth, viewed from above, is supposed to look like one of these balls made of twelve pieces of skin, variegated and marked out in different colors, of which the colors which we know are only limited samples, like the paints which artists use, but there the whole earth is made up of such colors, and others far brighter and purer still. One section is a marvelously beautiful purple, and another is golden. All that is white of it is whiter than chalk or snow, and the rest is similarly made up of the other colors, still more and lovelier than those which we have seen. Even these very hollows in the earth, full of water and air, assume a kind of color as they gleam amid the different hues around them, so that there appears to be one continuous surface of varied colors. The trees and flowers and fruits which grow upon this earth are proportionately beautiful. The mountains too and the stones have a proportionate smoothness and transparency, and their colors are lovelier. The pebbles which are so highly prized in our world — the jaspers and rubies and emeralds and the rest — are fragments of these stones, but there everything is as beautiful as they are, or better still. This is because the stones there are in their natural state, not damaged by decay and corroded by salt water as ours are by the sediment which has collected here, and which causes disfigurement and disease to stones and earth, and animals and plants as well. The earth itself is adorned not only with all these stones but also with gold and silver and the other metals, for many rich veins of them occur in plain view in all parts of the earth, so that to see them is a sight for the eyes of the blessed.

There are many kinds of animals upon it, and also human beings, some of whom live inland, others round the air, as we live round the sea, and others in islands surrounded by air but close to the mainland. In a word, as water and the sea are to us for our purposes, so is air to them, and as air is to us, so the aether is to them. Their climate is so temperate that they are free from disease and live much longer than people do here, and in sight and hearing and understanding and all other faculties they are as far superior to us as air is to water or aether to air in clarity.

They also have sanctuaries and temples which are truly inhabited by gods, and oracles and prophecies and visions and all other kinds of communion with the gods occur there face to face. They see the sun and moon and stars as they really are, and the rest of their happiness is after the same manner.

Such is the nature of the earth as a whole and of the things that are upon it. In the earth itself, all over its surface, there are many hollow regions, some deeper and more widely spread than that in which we live, others deeper than our region but with a smaller expanse, some both shallower than ours and broader. All these are joined together underground by many connection channels, some narrower, some wider, through which, from one basin to another, there flows a great volume of water—monstrous unceasing subterranean rivers of waters both hot and cold—and of fire too, great rivers of fire, and many of liquid mud, some clearer, some more turbid, like the rivers in Sicily that flow mud before the lava comes, and the lava stream itself. By these the several regions are filled in turn as the flood reaches them.

All this movement to and fro is caused by an oscillation inside the earth, and this oscillation is brought about by natural means, as follows.

One of the cavities in the earth is not only larger than the rest, but pierces right through from one side to the other. It is of this that Homer speaks when he says, "Far, far away, where lies earth's deepest chasm,"[1] while elsewhere both he and many other poets refer to it as Tartarus. Into this gulf all the rivers flow together, and from it they flow forth again, and each acquires the nature of that part of the earth through which it flows. The cause of the flowing in and out of all these streams is that the mass of liquid has no bottom or foundation; so it oscillates and surges to and for, and the air or breath that belongs to it does the same, for it accompanies the liquid both as it rushes to the further side of the earth and as it returns to this. And just as when we breathe we exhale and inhale the breath in a continuous stream, so in this case too the breath, oscillating with the liquid, causes terrible and monstrous winds as it passes in and out. So when the water retires to the so-called lower region the streams in the earth flow into those parts and irrigate them fully, and when in turn it ebbs from there and rushes back this way, it fills our streams again, and when they are filled they flow through their channels and through the earth; and arriving in those regions to which their ways have been severally prepared, they make seas and lakes and rivers and springs. Then sinking again beneath the ground, some by way of more and further regions, others by fewer and nearer, they empty themselves once more into Tartarus, some much lower, some only a little lower than the point at which they were emitted, but they all flow in at a level deeper than their rise. Some flow in on the opposite side to that on which they came out, and others on the same side, while some make a complete circle and, winding like a snake one or even more times round the earth, descend as far as possible before they again discharge their waters. It is possible to descend in either direction as far as the center,

1. *Iliad* 8.14.

but no further, for either direction from the center is uphill, which-
ever way the streams are flowing.

Among these many various mighty streams there are four in particular. The greatest of these, and the one which describes the outermost circle, is that which is called Oceanus. Directly opposite to this
and with a contrary course is Acheron, which not only flows through
other desolate regions but passes underground and arrives at the Acherusian Lake, where the souls of the dead for the most part come, and
after staying there for certain fixed periods, longer or shorter, are sent
forth again to the births of living creatures. Halfway between these
two a third river has its rise, and near its source issues into a great
place burning with sheets of fire, where it forms a boiling lake of muddy
water greater than our sea. From there it follows a circular course,
flowing turbid and muddy, and as it winds round inside the earth it
comes at last to the margin of the Acherusian Lake, but does not mingle
with the waters, and after many windings underground, it plunges
into Tartarus at a lower point. This is the river called Pyriphlegethon,
whose fiery stream belches forth jets of lava here and there in all parts
of the world. Directly opposite to this in its turn the fourth river breaks
out, first, they say, into a wild and dreadful place, all leaden gray,
which is called the Stygian region, and the lake which the river forms
on its entry is called Styx. After falling into this, and acquiring mysterious powers in its waters, the river passes underground and follows
a spiral course contrary to that of Pyriphlegethon, which it meets from
the opposite direction in the Acherusian Lake. This river too mingles
its stream with no other waters, but circling round falls into Tartarus
opposite Pyriphlegethon, and its name, the poets say, is Cocytus.

Such is the conformation of the earth and its rivers. And when
the newly dead reach the place to which each is conducted by his guardian spirit, first they submit to judgment, both those who have lived
well and holily, and those who have not. Those who are judged to
have lived a neutral life set out for Acheron, and embarking in those
vessels which await them, are conveyed in them to the lake, and there
they dwell, and undergoing purification are both absolved by punishment from any sins that they have committed, and rewarded for their
good deeds, according to each man's deserts. Those who on account
of the greatness of their sins are judged to be incurable, as having committed many gross acts of sacrilege or many wicked and lawless mur-
ders or any other such crimes — these are hurled by their appropriate
destiny into Tartarus, from whence they emerge no more.

Others are judged to have been guilty of sins which, though great, are curable — if, for example, they have offered violence to father or mother in a fit of passion, but spent the rest of their lives in penitence, or if they have committed manslaughter after the same fashion. These too must be cast into Tartarus, but when this has been done and they have remained there for a year, the surge casts them out — the man-slayers down Cocytus and the offenders against their parents down Pyriphlegethon. And when, as they are swept along, they come past the Acherusian Lake, there they cry aloud and call upon those whom they have killed or misused, and calling, beg and entreat for leave to pass from the stream into the lake, and be received by them. If they prevail, they come out and there is an end of their distress, but if not, they are swept away once more into Tartarus and from there back into the rivers, and find no release from their sufferings until they prevail upon those whom they have wronged, for this is the punishment which their judge has appointed for them.

But those who are judged to have lived a life of surpassing holi-ness — these are they who are released and set free from confinement in these regions of the earth, and passing upward to their pure abode, make their dwelling upon the earth's surface. And of these such as have purified themselves sufficiently by philosophy live thereafter altogether without bodies, and reach habitations even more beautiful, which it is not easy to portray — nor is there time to do so now. But the reasons which we have already described provide ground enough, as you can see, Simmias, for leaving nothing undone to attain during life some measure of goodness and wisdom, for the prize is glorious and the hope great.

Fustel de Coulanges
from The Ancient City, Chapter IV

The City
CIVITAS, and URBS, either of which we translate by the word *city*, were not synonymous words among the ancients. *Civitas* was the

religious and political association of families and tribes; *Urbs* was the place of assembly, the dwelling-place, and, above all, the sanctuary of this association.

We are not to picture ancient cities to ourselves as anything like what we see in our day. We build a few houses; it is a village. Insensibly the number of houses increases, and it becomes a city; and finally, if there is occasion for it, we surround this with a wall.

With the ancients, a city was never formed by degrees, by the slow increase of the number of men and houses. They founded a city at once, all entire in a day; but the elements of the city needed to be first ready, and this was the most difficult, and ordinarily the largest work. As soon as the families, the phratries, and the tribes had agreed to unite and have the same worship, they immediately founded the city as a sanctuary for this common worship, and thus the foundation of a city was always a religious act.

As a first example, we will take Rome itself, notwithstanding the doubt that is attached to its early history. It has often been said that Romulus was chief of a band of adventurers, and that he formed a people by calling around him vagabonds and robbers, and that all these men, collected without distinction, built at hazard a few huts to shelter their booty; but ancient writers present the facts in quite another shape, and it seems to us that if we desire to understand antiquity, our first rule should be to support ourselves upon the evidence that comes from the ancients. Those writers do, indeed, mention an asylum — that is to say, a sacred enclosure, where Romulus admitted all who presented themselves; and in this he followed the example which many founders of cities had afforded him. But this asylum was not the city; it was not even opened till after the city had been founded and completely built. It was an appendage added to Rome, but was not Rome. It did not even form a part of the city of Romulus; for it was situated at the foot of the Capitoline hill, whilst the city occupied the Palatine. It is of the first importance to distinguish the double element of the Roman population. In the asylum are adventurers without land or religion; on the Palatine are men from Alba — that is to say, men already organized into a society, distributed into *gentes* and curies, having a domestic worship and laws. The asylum is merely a hamlet or suburb, where the huts are built at hazard, and without rule; on the Palatine rises a city, religious and holy.

As to the manner in which this city was founded, antiquity abounds in information; we find it in Dionysius of Halicarnassus, who collected it from authors older than his time; we find it in Plutarch, in the *Fasti* of Ovid, in Tacitus, in Cato the Elder, who had consulted the ancient annals; and in two other writers who ought above all to inspire us with great confidence, the learned Varro and the learned Verrius Flaccus, whom Festus has preserved in part for us, both men deeply versed in Roman antiquities, lovers of truth, in no wise credulous, and well acquainted with the rules of historical criticism. All these writers have transmitted to us the tradition of the religious ceremony which marked the foundation of Rome, and we are not prepared to reject so great a number of witnesses.

It is not a rare thing for the ancients to relate facts that surprise us; but is this a reason why we should pronounce them fables? above all, if these facts, though not in accord with modern ideas, agree perfectly with those of the ancients? We have seen in their private life a religion which regulated all their acts; later, we saw that this religion established them in communities: why does it astonish us, after this, that the foundation of a city was a sacred act, and that Romulus himself was obliged to perform rites which were observed everywhere? The first care of the founder was to choose the site for the new city. But this choice — a weighty question, on which they believed the destiny of the people depended — was always left to the decision of the gods. If Romulus had been a Greek, he would have consulted the oracle of Delphi; if a Samnite, he would have followed the sacred animal — the wolf, or the green woodpecker. Being a Latin, and a neighbor of the Etruscans, initiated into the augurial science,[1] he asks the gods to reveal their will to him by the flight of birds. The gods point out the Palatine.

The day for the foundation having arrived, he first offers a sacrifice. His companions are ranged around him; they light a fire of brushwood, and each one leaps through the flame.[2] The explanation of this rite is, that for the act about to take place, it is necessary that the people be pure; and the ancients believed they could purify themselves from all stain, physical or moral, by leaping through a sacred flame.

When this preliminary ceremony had prepared the people for the grand act of the foundation, Romulus dug a small trench, of a circular form, and threw into it a clod of earth, which he had brought from the city of Alba.[3] Then each of his companions, approaching by turns, following his example, threw in a little earth, which he had brought from the country from which he had come. This rite is remarkable, and reveals to us a notion of the ancients to which we must call attention. Before coming to the Palatine, they had lived in Alba, or some other neighboring city. There was their sacred fire; there their fathers had lived and been buried. Now, their religion forbade them to quit the land where the hearth had been established, and where their divine ancestors reposed. It was necessary, then, in order to be free from all impiety, that each of these men should employ a fiction, and that he should carry with him, under the symbol of a clod of earth, the sacred soil where his ancestors were buried, and to which their manes were attached. A man could not quit his dwelling-place without taking with him his soil and his ancestors. This rite had to be accomplished, so that he might say, pointing out the new place which he had adopted, This is still the land of my fathers, *terra patrum, patria;* here is my country, for here are the manes of my family.

The trench into which each one had thrown a little earth was called *mundus.* Now, this word designated in the ancient language, the region of the manes.[4] From this place, according to tradition, the souls of the dead escaped three times a year, desirous of again seeing the light for a moment. Do we not see also, in this tradition, the real thought of these ancient men? When placing in the trench a clod of earth from their former country, they believed they had enclosed there the souls of their ancestors. These souls, reunited there, required a perpetual worship, and kept guard over their descendants. At this same place Romulus set up an altar, and lighted a fire upon it. This was the holy fire of the city.[5]

Around this hearth arose the city, as the house rises around the domestic hearth; Romulus traced a furrow which marked the enclosure. Here, too, the smallest details were fixed by a ritual. The founder made use of a copper ploughshare; his plough was drawn by a white bull and a white cow. Romulus, with his head veiled, and in the priestly robes, himself held the handle of the plough and directed it, while chanting prayers. His companions followed him, observing a religious silence. As the plough turned up clods of earth, they carefully threw them within the enclosure, that no particle of this sacred earth should be on the side of the stranger.[6] This enclosure, traced by religion, was inviolable. Neither stranger nor citizen had the right to cross over it. To leap over this little furrow was an impious act; it is a Roman tradition that the founder's brother committed this act of sacrilege, and paid for it with his life.[7]

But, in order that men might enter and leave the city, the furrow was interrupted in certain places.[8] To accomplish this, Romulus raised the plough and carried it over; these intervals were called *portae;* these were the gates of the city.

Upon the sacred furrow, or a little inside of it, the walls afterwards arose; they also were sacred.[9] No one could touch them, even to repair them, without permission from the pontiffs. On both sides of this wall a space, a few paces wide, was given up to religion, and was called the *pomaerium;*[10] on this space no plough could be used, no building constructed.

Such, according to a multitude of ancient witnesses, was the ceremony of the foundation of Rome. If it is asked how this information was preserved down to the writers who have transmitted it to us, the answer is, that the ceremony was recalled to the memory of the people every year by an anniversary festival, which they called the birthday of Rome. This festival was celebrated through all antiquity, from year to year, and the Roman people still celebrate it today, at the same date as formerly — the 21st of April. So faithful are men to old usages through incessant changes.

We cannot reasonably suppose that such rites were observed for the first time by Romulus. It is certain, on the contrary, that many cities, before Rome, had been founded in the same manner. According to Varro, these rites were common to Latium and Etruria. Cato the Elder, who, in order to write his *Origines,* had consulted the annals of all the Italian nations, informs us that analogous rites were practised by all founders of cities. The Etruscans possessed liturgical books in which were recorded the complete ritual of these ceremonies.[11]

The Greeks, like the Italians, believed that the site of a city should be chosen and revealed by the divinity. So, when they wished to found one, they consulted the oracle at Delphi.[12] Herodotus records, as an act of impiety or madness, that the Spartan Dorieus dared to build a city "without consulting the oracle, and without observing any of the customary usages;" and the pious historian is not surprised that a city thus constructed in despite of the rules lasted only three years.[13] Thucydides, recalling the day when Sparta was founded, mentions the pious chants, and the sacrifices of that day. The same historian tells us that the Athenians had a particular ritual, and that they never founded a colony without conforming to it.[14] We may see in a comedy of Aristophanes a sufficiently exact picture of the ceremony practised in such cases. When the poet represented the amusing foundation of the city of the birds, he certainly had in mind the customs which were observed in the foundation of the cities of men. Now he puts upon the scene a priest who lighted a fire while invoking the gods, a poet who sang hymns, and a divine who recited oracles.

Notes

1. Cicero, *De Divin.*, I. 17. Plutarch, *Camillus*, 32. Pliny, XIV. 2; XVIII. 12.

2. Dionysius, I. 88.

3. Plutarch, *Romulus*, 11. Dion Cassius, *Fragm.*, 12. Ovid, *Fasti*, IV. 821. Festus, v. *Quadrata.*

4. Festus, v. *Mundus.* Servius, *ad Aen.*, III. 134. Plutarch, *Romulus*, 11.

5. Ovid, *ibid.* Later the hearth was removed. When the three cities, the Palatine, the Capitoline, and the Quirinal were united in one, the common hearth, or temple of Vesta, was placed on neutral ground between the three hills.

6. Plutarch, *Romulus*, 11. Ovid, *Ibidem.* Varro, *De Ling. Lat.*, V. 143. Festus, v. *Primigenius; v. Urvat.* Virgil, V. 755.

7. See Plutarch, *Rom. Quest.*, 27.

8. Cato, in *Servius, V.* 755.

9. Cicero, *De Nat. Deor.*, III. 40. *Digest*, 8, 8. Gaius, II. 8.

10. Varro, V. 143. Livy, I. 44. Aulus Gellius XIII. 14.

11. Cato, in Servius, V. 755. Varro, *L. L.*, V. 143. Festus, v. *Rituales.*

12. Diodorus, XII. 12; Pausanias, VII. 2. Athenaeus, VIII. 62.

13. Herodotus, V. 42.

14. Thucydides, V. 16; III. 24.

Gerardus Mercator

A letter written to Mr. Richard Hakluyt of Oxford

touching the intended discovery of the Northeast Passage

(1580)

Sir, I wish Arthur Pet had been informed before his departure of some special points. The voyage to Cathay by the east is doubtless very easy and short, and I have oftentimes marvelled, that being so happily begun, it hath been left off, and the course changed into the west, after that more than half of your voyage was discovered. For beyond Novaya Zemlya there followeth presently a great bay, which on the left side is enclosed with the mighty promontory Tabin. Into the midst hereof fall great rivers, which passing through the whole country of Serica, and being as I think navigable with great vessels into the heart of the continent, may be an easy means whereby to traffic for all manner of merchandise, and transport them out of Cathay, and other kingdoms thereabouts into England. But considering with myself that that navigation was not intermitted, but upon great occasion, I thought that the Emperor of Russia and Muscovy had hindered the proceeding thereof. If so be that with his grace and favour a further navigation may be made, I would counsel them certainly to search this bay and rivers aforesaid, and in them to pick and choose out some convenient port and harbour for the English merchants, from whence afterward with more opportunity and less peril all the coast of Cathay may be discovered. That the pole of the loadstone is not far beyond I have learned by the certain observations of the loadstone: about which pole I think there are very many rocks, and very hard and dangerous sailing: and yet a more hard and difficult passage I think it to be this way which is now attempted by the west, for it is nearer to the pole of the loadstone, to the which I think it not safe to approach. And because the loadstone hath another pole than that of the world, the nearer you come unto it, the more the needle of the compass doth vary from the north, sometimes to the west, and sometimes to the east, according as a man is to the eastward or to the westward of that meridian.

This is a strange alteration and very apt to deceive the sailor, unless he know the unconstancy and variation of the compass, and take the elevation of the pole sometimes with his instruments. If Master Arthur be not well provided in this behalf, or of such dexterity, that perceiving the error he be not able to correct the same, I fear lest in wandering up and down he lose his time, and be overtaken with the ice in the midst of the enterprise. For that gulf, as they say, is frozen every year very hard.

Thomas Burnet
from The Sacred Theory of the Earth

*Concerning the Mountains of the Earth, their greatness and
irregular Form, their Situation, Causes, and Origin.*

We have been in the hollows of the Earth, and the Chambers of the
Deep, amongest the damps and steams of those lower Regions; let us
now go air our selves on the tops of the Mountains, where we shall
have a more free and large Horizon, and quite another face of things
will present it self to our observation.

The greatest objects of Nature are, methinks, the most pleasing
to behold; and next to the great Concave of the Heavens, and those
boundless Regions where the Stars inhabit, there is nothing that I look
upon with more pleasure than the wide Sea and the Mountains of the
Earth. There is something august and stately in the Air of these things,
that inspires the mind with great thoughts and passions; We do naturally, upon such occasions, think of God and his greatness: and what-
soever hath but the shadow and appearance of INFINITE, as all things
have that are too big for our comprehension, they fill and over-bear
the mind with their Excess, and cast it into a pleasing kind of stupor
and admiration.

And yet these Mountains we are speaking of, to confess the truth,
are nothing but great ruines; but such as show a certain magnificence
in Nature; as from old Temples and broken Amphitheaters of the
Romans we collect the greatness of that people. But the grandeur of
a Nation is less sensible to those that never see the remains and monuments they have left, and those who never see the mountainous parts
of the Earth, scarce ever reflect upon the causes of them, or what power
in Nature could be sufficient to produce them. The truth is, the gener-
ality of people have not sence and curiosity enough to raise a question concerning these things, or concerning the Original of them. You
may tell them that Mountains grow out of the Earth like Fuzz-balls,
or that there are Monsters under ground that throw up Mountains
as Moles do Mole-hills; they will scarce raise one objection against
your doctrine; or if you would appear more Learned, tell them that
the Earth is a great Animal, and these are Wens that grow upon its
body. This would pass current for Philosophy; so much is the World
drown'd in stupidity and sensual pleasures, and so little inquisitive

into the works of God and Nature.

There is nothing doth more awaken our thoughts or excite our minds to enquire into the causes of such things, than the actual view of them; as I have had experience my self when it was my fortune to cross the *Alps* and *Appennine* Mountains; for the sight of those wild, vast and indigested heaps of Stones and Earth, did so deeply strike my fancy, that I was not easie till I could give my self some tolerable account how that confusion came in Nature. 'Tis true, the height of Mountains compar'd with the Diameter of the Earth is not considerable, but the extent of them and the ground they stand upon, bears a considerable proportion to the surface of the Earth; and if from *Europe* we may take our measures for the rest, I easily believe, that the Mountains do at least take up the tenth part of the dry land. The Geographers are not very careful to describe or note in their Charts, the multitude or situation of Mountains; They mark the bounds of Countries, the site of Cities and Towns, and the course of Rivers, because these are things of chief use to civil affairs and commerce, and that they design to serve and not Philosophy or Natural History. But *Cluverius* in his description of *Ancient Germany*, *Switzerland* and *Italy*, hath given Maps of those Countries more approaching to the natural face of them, and we have drawn (at the end of this Chapter) such a Map of either Hemisphere, without marking Countries or Towns, or any such artificial things; distinguishing only Land and Sea, Islands and Continents, Mountains and not Mountains; and 'tis very useful to imagine the Earth in this manner, and to look often upon such bare draughts as shew us Nature undrest; for then we are best able to judge what her true shapes and proportions are.

As for Subterraneous things, Metals and Minerals, I believe they had none in the first Earth; and the happier they; no Gold, nor Silver, nor courser Metals. The use of these is either imaginary, or in such works, as, by the constitution of their World, they had little occasion for. And Minerals are either for Medicine, which they had no need of further than Herbs; or for Materials to certain Arts, which were not then in use, or were suppli'd by other ways. These Subterraneous things, Metals and metallick Minerals, are Factitious, not Original bodies, coeval with the Earth; but are made in process of time, after long preparations and concoctions, by the action of the Sun within the bowels of the Earth. And if the *Stamina* or principles of them rise from the lower Regions that lie under the Abysse, as I am apt to think they do, it doth not seem probable, that they could be drawn through such a mass of Waters, or that the heat of the Sun could on a sudden penetrate so deep, and be able to loosen them, and raise them into the exterior Earth. And as the first Age of the World was call'd *Golden*, though it knew not what Gold was; so the following Ages had their names from several Metals, which lay then asleep in the dark and deep womb of Nature, and see not the Sun till many Years and Ages afterwards.

There is another thing in Antiquity, relating to the form and construction of the Earth, which is very remarkable, and hath obtain'd throughout all learned Nations and Ages. And that is the comparisons or resemblance of the Earth to an *Egg*. And this is not so much for its External Figure, though that be true too: as for the inward composition of it; consisting of several Orbs, one including another, and in that order, as to answer the several Elementary Regions of which the new-made Earth was constituted. For if we admit for the *Yolk* a Central fire (which, though very reasonable, we had no occasion to take notice of in our Theory of the Chaos) and suppose the Figure of the Earth *Oval*, and a little extended towards the Poles, as probably it was; those two bodies do very naturally represent one another; as in this Scheme, which represents the Interiour faces of both, a divided *Egg*, or Earth. Where, as the two inmost Regions A. B. represent the Yolk and the Membrane that lies next about it; so the Exteriour Region of the Earth (D) is as the Shell of the Egg, and the Abysse (C) under it as the White that lies under the Shell. And considering that this notion of the *Mundane Egg*, or that the World was *Oviform*, hath been the sence and Language of all Antiquity, *Latins*, *Greeks*, *Persians*, *Egyptians*, and others, as we have shew'd elsewhere; I thought it worthy our notice in this place; seeing it receives such a clear and easie explication from that Origin and Fabrick we have given to the first Earth, and also reflects light upon the Theory it self, and confirms it to be no fiction: This notion, which is a kind of Epitome or Image of it, having been conserv'd in the most ancient Learning.

G.W.F. Hegel
from Introduction to the Philosophy of History
translated by J. Sibree

Geographical Basis of History

Contrasted with the universality of the moral Whole and with the unity of that individuality which is its active principle, the *natural* connection that helps to produce the Spirit of a People, appears an extrinsic element; but inasmuch as we must regard it as the ground on which that Spirit plays its part, it is an *essential* and *necessary* basis. We begin with the assertion that, in the History of the World, the Idea of Spirit appears in its actual embodiment as a series of external forms, each one of which declares itself as an actually existing people. This existence falls under the category of Time as well as Space, in the way of natural existence; and the special principle, which every world-historical people embodies, has this principle at the same time as a *natural* characteristic. Spirit, clothing itself in this form of nature, suffers its particular phases to assume separate existence; for mutual exclusion is the mode of existence proper to mere nature. These natural distinctions must be first of all regarded as special possibilities, from which the Spirit of the people in question germinates, and among them is the Geographical Basis. It is not our concern to become acquainted with the land occupied by nations as an external locale, but with the natural type of the locality, as intimately connected with the type and character of the people which is the offspring of such a soil. This character is nothing more nor less than the mode and form in which nations make their appearance in History, and take place and position in it. Nature should not be rated too high nor too low: the mild Ionic sky certainly contributed much to the charm of the Homeric poems, yet this alone can produce no Homers. Nor in fact does it continue to produce them; under Turkish government no bards have arisen. We must first take notice of those natural conditions which have to be excluded once for all from the drama of the World's History. In the Frigid and in the Torrid zone the locality of World-historical people cannot be found. For awakening consciousness takes its rise surrounded by natural influences alone, and every development of it is the reflection of Spirit back upon itself in opposition to the immediate, unreflected character of mere nature. Nature is therefore one element in this antithetic abstracting process; Nature is the first stand point from which man can gain freedom within himself, and this liberation must not be rendered difficult by natural obstructions. Nature, as contrasted with Spirit, is a quantitative mass, whose power must not be so great as to make its single force omnipotent. In the extreme zones man cannot come to free movement; cold and heat are here too powerful to allow Spirit to build up a world for *itself*. Aristotle said long ago, "When pressing needs are satisfied, man turns to the general and more elevated." But in the extreme zones such pressure may be said never to cease, never to be warded off; men are constantly impelled to direct attention to nature, to the glowing rays of the sun, and the icy frost. The true theatre of History is therefore the temperate zone; or rather, its northern half, because the earth there presents itself in a continental form, and has a broad breast, as the Greeks say. In the south, on the contrary, it divides itself, and runs out into many points. The same peculiarity shews itself in natural products. The north has many kinds of animals and plants with common characteristics; in the south, where the land divides itself into points, natural forms also present individual features contrasted with each other.

The World is divided into *Old* and *New*; the name of *New* having originated in the fact that America and Australia have only lately become known to us. But these parts of the world are not only relatively new, but intrinsically so in respect of their entire physical and psychical constitution. Their geological antiquity we have nothing to do with. I will not deny the New World the honour of having emerged from the sea at the world's formation contemporaneously with the old: yet the Archipelago between South America and Asia shews a physical immaturity. The greater part of the islands are so constituted, that they are, as it were, only a superficial deposit of earth over rocks, which shoot up from the fathomless deep, and bear the character of novel origination. New Holland shows a not less immature geographical character: for in penetrating from the settlements of the English farther into the country, we discover immense streams, which have not yet developed themselves to such a degree as to dig a channel for themselves, but lose themselves in marshes. Of America and its grade of civilization, especially in Mexico and Peru, we have information, but it imports nothing more than that this culture was an entirely national one, which must expire as soon as Spirit approached it. America has always shewn itself physically and psychically powerless, and still shews itself so. For the aborigines, after the landing of the Europeans in American, gradually vanished at the breath of European activity. In the United States of North America all the citizens are of European descent, with whom the old inhabitants could not amalgamate, but were driven back. The aborigines have certainly adopted some arts and usages from the Europeans, among others that of brandy-drinking, which has operated with deadly effect. In the South the natives were treated with much greater violence, and employed in hard labours to which their strength was by no means competent. A mild and passionless disposition, want of spirit, and a crouching submissiveness towards a Creole, and still more towards a European, are the chief characteristics of the native Americans; and it will be long before the Europeans succeed in producing any independence of feeling in them. The inferiority of these individuals in all respects, even in regard to size, is very manifest; only the quite southern races in Patagonia are more vigorous natures, but still abiding in their natural condition of rudeness and barbarism. When the Jesuits and the Catholic clergy proposed to accustom the Indians to European culture and manners (they have, as is well known, founded a state in Paraguay and convents in Mexico and California), they commenced a close intimacy with them, and prescribed for them the duties of the day, which slothful though their disposition was, they complied with under the authority of the Friars. These prescripts, (at midnight a bell had to remind them even of their matrimonial duties,) were first, and very wisely, directed to the creation of wants—the springs of human activity generally. The weakness of the American physique was a chief reason for bringing the negroes to America, to employ their labour in the work that had to be done in the New World; for the negroes are far more susceptible of European culture than the Indians, and an English traveller has adduced instances of negroes having become competent clergymen, medical men, etc. (a negro first discovered the use of the Peruvian bark), while only a single native was known to him whose intellect was sufficiently developed to enable him to study, but who had died soon after beginning, through excessive brandy-drinking. The weakness of the human physique of America has been aggravated by a deficiency in the mere tools and appliances of progress, — the want of *horses* and *iron*, the chief instruments by which they were subdued.

The original nation having vanished or nearly so, the effective population comes for the most part from Europe; and what takes place in America, is but an emanation from Europe. Europe has sent its surplus population to America in much the same way as from the old

Imperial Cities, where trade-guilds were dominant and trade was stereotyped, many persons escaped to other towns which were not under such a yoke, and where the burden of imposts was not so heavy. Thus arose, by the side of Hamburg, Altona, — by Frankfort, Offenbach, — by Nürnburg, Fürth, — and Carouge by Geneva. The relation between North America and Europe is similar. Many Englishmen have settled there, where burdens and imposts do not exist, and where the combination of European appliances and European ingenuity has availed to realize some produce from the extensive and still virgin soil. Indeed the emigration in question offers many advantages. The emigrants have got rid of much that might be obstructive to their interests at home, while they take with them the advantages of European independence of spirit, and acquired skill; while for those who are willing to work vigorously, but who have not found in Europe opportunities for doing so, a sphere of action is certainly presented in America.

America, as is well known, is divided into two parts, connected indeed by an isthmus, but which has not been the means of establishing intercourse between them. Rather, these two divisions are most decidedly distinct from each other. North America shews us on approaching it, along its eastern shore a wide border of level coast, behind which is stretched a chain of mountains — the blue mountains or Apalachians; further north the Alleghanies. Streams issuing from them water the country towards the coast, which affords advantages of the most desirable kind to the United States, whose origin belongs to this region. Behind that mountain-chain the St. Lawrence river flows, (in connection with huge lakes), from south to north, and on this river lie the northern colonies of Canada. Farther west we meet the basin of the vast Mississippi, and the basins of the Missouri and Ohio, which it receives, and then debouches into the bay of Mexico. On the western side of this region we have in like manner a long mountain chain, running through Mexico and the Isthmus of Panama, and under the names of the Andes or Cordillera, cutting off an edge of coast along the whole west side of South America. The border formed by this is narrower and offers fewer advantages than that of North America. There lie Peru and Chili. On the east side flow eastwards the monstrous streams of the Orinoco and Amazons; they form great valleys, not adapted however for cultivation, since they are only wide desert steppes. Towards the south flows the Rio de la Plata, whose tributaries have their origin partly in the Cordilleras, partly in the northern chain of mountains which separates the basin of the Amazons from its own. To the district of the Rio de la Plata belong Brazil, and the Spanish Republics. Columbia is the northern coast-land of South America, at the west of which, flowing along the Andes, the Magdalena debouches into the Caribbean Sea.

With the exception of Brazil, republics have come to occupy South as well as North America. In comparing South America (reckoning Mexico as part of it) with North America, we observe an astonishing contrast.

In North America we witness a prosperous state of things, an increase of industry and population, civil order and firm freedom; the whole federation constitutes but a single state, and has its political centres. In South America, on the contrary, the republics depend only on military force; their whole history is a continued revolution; federated states become disunited; others previously separated become united; and all these changes originate in military revolutions. The more special differences between the two parts of America shew us two opposite directions, the one in political respects, the other in regard to religion. South America, where the Spaniards settled and asserted supremacy, is Catholic; North America, although a land of sects of every name, is yet fundamentally, Protestant. A wider distinction is presented in the fact, that South America was conquered, but North America colonised. The Spaniards took possession of South America to govern it, and to become rich through occupying political offices, and by exactions. Depending on a very distant mother-country, their desires found a larger scope, and by force address and confidence they gained a great predominance over the Indians. The North American States, were, on the other hand, entirely *colonized*, by Europeans. Since in England Puritans, Episcopalians, and Catholics were engaged in perpetual conflict, and now one party, now the other had the upper hand, many emigrated to seek religious freedom on a foreign shore. These were industrious Europeans, who betook themselves to agriculture, tobacco and cotton planting, etc. Soon the whole attention of the inhabitants was given to labour, and the basis of their existence as a united body lay in the necessities that bind man to man, the desire of repose, the establishment of civil rights, security and freedom, and a community arising from the aggregation of individuals as atomic constituents; so that the state was merely something external for the protection of property. From the Protestant religion sprang the principle of the mutual confidence of individuals, — trust in the honourable dispositions of other men; for in the Protestant Church the entire life —

its activity generally — is the field for what it deems religious works. Among Catholics, on the contrary, the basis of such a confidence cannot exist; for in secular matters only force and voluntary subservience are the principles of action; and the forms which are called Constitutions are in this case only a resort of necessity, and are no protection against mistrust.

If we compare North America further with Europe, we shall find in the former the permanent example of a republican constitution. A subjective unity presents itself; for there is a President at the head of the State, who, for the sake of security against any monarchical ambition, is chosen only for four years. Universal protection for property, and a something approaching entire immunity from public burdens, are facts which are constantly held up to commendation. We have in these facts the fundamental character of the community, — the endeavour of the individual after acquisition, commercial profit, and gain; the preponderance of *private* interest, devoting itself to that of the community only for its own advantage. We find, certainly, legal relations — a formal code of laws; but respect for law exists apart from genuine probity, and the American merchants commonly lie under the imputation of dishonest dealings under legal protection. If, on the one side, the Protestant Church develops the essential principle of confidence, as already stated, it thereby involves on the other hand the recognition of the validity of the element of feeling to such a degree as gives encouragement to unseemly varieties of caprice. Those who adopt this stand-point maintain, that, as every one may have his peculiar way of viewing things *generally*, so he may have also a *religion* peculiar to himself. Thence the splitting up into so many sects, which reach the very acme of absurdity; many of which have a form of worship consisting in convulsive movements, and sometimes in the most sensuous extravagances. This complete freedom of worship is developed to such a degree, that the various congregations choose ministers and dismiss them according to their absolute pleasure; for the Church is no independent existence, — having a substantial spiritual being, and correspondingly permanent external arrangement, — but the affairs of religion are regulated by the good pleasure for the time being of the members of the community. In North America the most unbounded licence of imagination in religious matters prevails, and that religious unity is wanting which has been maintained in European States, where deviations are limited to a few confessions. As to the political condition of North America, the general object of the existence of this State is not yet fixed and determined, and the necessity for a firm combination does not yet exist; for a real State and a real Government arise only after a distinction of classes has arisen, when wealth and poverty become extreme, and when such a condition of things presents itself that a large portion of the people can no longer satisfy its necessities in the way in which it has been accustomed so to do. But America is hitherto exempt from this pressure, for it has the outlet of colonization constantly and widely open, and multitudes are continually streaming into the plains of the Mississippi. By this means the chief source of discontent is removed, and the continuation of the existing civil condition is guaranteed. A comparison of the United States of North America with European lands is therefore impossible; for in Europe, such a natural outlet for population, notwithstanding all the emigrations that take place, does not exist. Had the woods of Germany been in existence, the French Revolution would not have occurred. North America will be comparable with Europe only after the immeasurable space which that country presents to its inhabitants shall have been occupied, and the members of the political body shall have begun to be pressed back on each other. North America is still in the condition of having land to begin to cultivate. Only when, as in Europe, the direct increase of agriculturists is checked, will the inhabitants, instead of pressing outwards to occupy the fields, press inwards upon each other, —pursuing town occupations, and trading with their fellow citizens; and so form a compact system of civil society, and require an organized state. The North American Federation have no neighbouring State, (towards which they occupy a relation similar to that of European States to each other), one which they regard with mistrust, and against which they must keep up a standing army. Canada and Mexico are not objects of fear, and England has had fifty years experience, that *free* America is more profitable to her than it was in a state of *dependence*. The militia of the North American Republic proved themselves quite as brave in the War of Independence, as the Dutch under Philip II.; but generally, where Independence is not at stake, less power is displayed, and in the year 1814 the militia held out but indifferently against the English.

America is therefore the land of the future, where, in the ages that lie before us, the burden of the World's History shall reveal itself, — perhaps in a contest between North and South America. It is a land of desire for all those who are weary of the historical lumber-room of old Europe. Napoleon is reported to have said, *"Cette vieille Europe m'ennuie.''* It is for America to abandon the ground on which hitherto the History of the World has developed itself. What *has* taken place in the New World up to the present time is only an echo of the Old World, — the expression of a foreign Life; and as a Land of the Future, it has no interest for us here, for, as regards *History*, our concern must be with that which has been and that which is. In regard to *Philosophy*, on the other hand, we have to do with that which (strictly speaking) is neither past nor future, but with that which *is*, which has an eternal existence — with Reason; and this is quite sufficient to occupy us.

On the rudest surface of English earth, there is seen the effect of centuries of civilization, so that you do not quite get at naked Nature anywhere. And then every point of beauty is so well known, and has been described so much, that one must needs look through other people's eyes, and feel as if he were seeing a picture rather than a reality.
— Nathaniel Hawthorne, visiting the Lake district 1855

There was a foreboding of eternity in a yard of space.
— Fyodor Dostoevsky

I always have the feeling that nature — the air, leaves, rain — sees and understands everything, and wants to help — wants to help very much indeed, but cannot.   — Tertz

When Adam and Eve were cast out of the Garden of Eden, they were separated on the earth, and met only afterwards at a mountain near Mecca called by the Arabs Arafat, or The Recognition.
— Moslem Legend

Mahaprajna-paramita is a Sanskrit term of the western country; in the T'ang language it means: great-wisdom-other-shore-reached . . . What is Maha? Maha is great . . . What is Prajna? Prajna is wisdom . . . What is Paramita? The other shore reached . . . Oh gone, gone, gone, gone to the other shore, fallen on the other shore . . .

—quoted by Octavio Paz (Hui-neng, 7th c.)

I swear the earth shall surely be complete to him or her who shall
   be complete,
The earth remains jagged and broken only to him or her who
   remains jagged and broken.

I swear there is no greatness or power that does not emulate those
   of the earth,
There can be no theory of any account unless it corroborate the
   theory of the earth,
No politics, song, religion, behavior, or what not, is of account,
   unless it compare with the amplitude of the earth,
Unless it face the exactness, vitality, impartiality, rectitude of the
   earth.

Say on, sayers! sing on, singers!
Delve! mould! pile the words of the earth!
Work on, age after age, nothing is to be lost,
It may have to wait long, but it will certainly come in use,
When the materials are all prepared and ready, the architects
   shall appear.

—Walt Whitman, *A Song of the Rolling Earth*

In the East Indies it is said that a king should have a seat of loadstone at his coronation; probably because the magnetic influence of the stone was supposed to attract power, favor, and gifts to the sovereign. But it is not only in the Orient that magnetite is prized for its talismanic powers, for even in some parts of our own land this belief is still prevalent. Large quantities of loadstone are found at Magnet Cove, Arkansas, and it is estimated that from one to three tons are sold annually

to the negroes to be used in the Voodoo ceremonies as conjuring stones. The material has been found in land used for farming purposes, and many pieces have been turned up in ploughing for corn; these vary from the size of a pea to masses weighing from ten to twenty pounds. They occur in a reddish-brown, sticky soil; their surface is smooth and brown and they have the appearance of water-worn pebbles. In July, 1887, an interesting case was tried in Macon, Georgia, where a negro woman sued a conjurer to recover five dollars which she had paid him for a piece of loadstone to serve as a charm to bring back her wandering husband. As the market value of this mineral was only seventy-five cents a pound, and the piece was very small, weighing but a few ounces, the judge ordered that the money should be refunded.
—George Kunz, *The Curious Lore of Precious Stones*

On Rigor in Science
. . . In that Empire, the Art of Cartography reached such Perfection that the map of one Province alone took up the whole of a City, and the map of the Empire, the whole of a Province. In time, even those unconscionable Maps grew unsatisfactory, and the Schools of Cartographers created a Map of the Empire that was the size of the Empire itself, and coincided with it point to point. The succeeding Generations, less addicted to the Study of Cartography, became aware that this University Map was Worthless, and, not without Impiety, they abandoned it to the Inclemencies of the Sun and of the Winters. In the Deserts of the West some mangled Ruins of the Map wore on, inhabited by Animals and Beggars; in the whole Country there are no other relics of the Sciences of Geography.
—Suarez Miranda, *Viajes de Varones Prudentes*, Bk 4, Ch XLV, Lerida, 1658 (in Borges, "Museum")

It doesn't matter how much you read history—you may accept it but you can't really know and feel it. To actually touch those objects was another experience altogether—the knives, forks, boots, stoneware, bottles that still looked as new as the day they were brought ashore— these were my inspiration. I could feel an incredible tension in the place, which produced strong emotions within me. Any disaster site where a number of people died quickly has that feeling, particularly when

they were young people.
—Peter Weir, on seeing the abandoned Gallipoli battlefields of World War One, preserved because they have remained a Turkish military zone.

I shall now tell the story of Zarathustra. The basic conception of the work, the *idea of eternal recurrence*, the highest formula of affirmation that can possibly be attained—belongs to the August of the year 1881: it was jotted down on a piece of paper with the inscription: "6000 feet beyond man and time." I was that day walking through the woods beside the lake of Silvaplana; I stopped beside a mighty pyramidal block of stone which reared itself up not far from Surlei. Then this idea came to me.   —Friedrich Nietzsche, *Ecce Homo*

The Palace is not infinite.

The walls, the embankments, the gardens, the labyrinths, the steps, the terraces, the parapets, the doors, the galleries, the circular or rectangular courtyards, the cloisters, the crossroads, the cisterns, the antechambers, the chambers, the alcoves, the libraries, the garrets, the prisons, the cells without exit, and the underground vaults, are no less numerous than the grains of sand of the Ganges, but their number has an end. He is not absent who can, from the flat roofs, make out toward the west the smithies, the carpenters' shops, the stables, the shipyards, and the hovels of slaves.

To no one is it given to travel through more than an infinitesimal part of the Palace. Some are acquainted with no more than the cellars. We are able to perceive some faces, some voices, some words, but what we perceive is the most inferior. Inferior and precious at once. The date that the steel engraves on the tablet, that the parish registers record, is later than our death. We are dead already when nothing touches us, neither a word nor a longing nor a memory. I know that I am not dead.   —Jorge Luis Borges (translated by Thomas Frick)

Men are born either Catastrophists or Uniformitarians. You may divide the race into imaginative people who believe in all sorts of impending crises—physical, social, political—and others who anchor their very souls *in status quo*. There are men who build arks straight thru their natural lives ready for the first sprinkle, and there are others who do not watch Old Probabilities or even own an umbrella.

—Clarence King, *Catastrophism and the Evolution of Environment,*

Land has grown, the sky has grown, and the ocean has grown; all these are filled with living creatures. The room for gods is filled with gods, and now what shall be done for the room for people?

—Tahitian legend recorded in 1822, Douglas Oliver, *Ancient Tahitian Society*

Long before the coming of the white man, mother bear Mishe-Mokwa and her twin cubs were driven from the shores of Wisconsin by fire and famine into the waters of Lake Michigan. The three had no other choice but to set out swimming for the far distant shoreline of Michigan. The journey seemed impossible, and fear inhabited their hearts. After many days without rest in the water, the Michigan shoreline came into view. However, the extreme effort had by that time taken its toll, and exhaustion caused the two cubs to succumb, one at a time, to the call of the blue waters. Within reach of shore, Mishe-Mokwa, ravaged by her inability to save her cubs so close to the end of the journey, dragged herself upon the virgin land and tore savagely at the woodland shoreline, creating the great bare sand dune as a memorial, under which she lies in restless sleep. The god Manitou, responding to Mishe-Mokwa's deep love and longing, made her two cubs rise up from the depths to form islands within sight of the shore. They are named North and South Manitou in his honor.   —[Postcard]

The growing number of travelers enjoying the Dempster highway's wilderness has ignited a significant environmental debate. Essentially, it pits those eager to preserve existing wildlife and rural native lifestyles and values against resource and business forces that see the road as a vital land link in allowing Canada's isolated Northerners to enjoy the same kind of growth and development as their Southern countrymen.

A major issue concerns the Porcupine Caribou Herd, with 110,000 animals one of the world's last large wild herds. The caribou's migrations across a 200 mile front take them directly toward the Dempster, which many fear creates a physical and psychological barrier for these skittish creatures.

For two years now the herd has not crossed the new road. A major study is under way to determine why, as well as what protective measures, such as closing the highway during migration times, might be necessary. —*The New York Times*

I conceived a room filled with wet sand mixed in with one-dollar bills, in which I would burrow, digging tunnels and reinforcing them with plywood panels. I would then try to remain hidden in the tunnels while I would invite persons to try & uncover me. Allowing that they might keep whatever they uncovered. —Michael Metz

Out of this blackness, nature's unfathomed treasure house, man must exhume the stone of his own soul in the same way that the miner removes the diamond from its sheath of black carbon.
—Manly P. Hall

Say, you are in the country; in some high land of lakes. Take almost any path you please, and ten to one it carries you down in a dale, and leaves you there by a pool in the stream. There is magic in it.
—Herman Melville, *Moby Dick*

Lars Gustafsson

Ballad on the Paths in Vastmänland

translated by Yvonne Sandström

Beneath the visible writing of small roads,
gravel roads, forest roads, often with a crest
of grass in the center, between sunken wheeltracks,
hidden by brush piles from clear-cuttings,
still evident in the dried-up moss,
there is a different writing: the old paths.
They lead from lake to lake, valley
to valley. Sometimes they deepen,
become quite evident, are carried by solid bridges
of medieval stone across black-water brooks,
sometimes they peter out over naked rock,
it's easy to lose them in the marshes, they're
so unremarkable that they're there one moment, gone
the next. There's a continuation, there's
always a continuation, if only
you keep looking, these paths are stubborn,
they know what they want and added
to that knowledge is considerable guile.
You're walking eastward, your compass points east with
                                      stubborn zeal,
the path follows the compass faithfully, like a line,
everything is in order, then the path turns north.
There's nothing to the north. What does the path want now?
Soon a huge bog appears, and the path knew it.
It carries us around, with the confidence of someone
who's been there before. It knows the whereabouts of the bog,
knows where the mountain grows too steep, knows
what happens to someone walking north of the lake

Translations from *Artesian Wells, Cartesian Dreams* (1980)

instead of south. It's done it all
so many times before. That's the whole point
of being a path. That it's been done
before. Who made the path? Charcoal-burners, fishermen,
women with skinny arms who gathered wood?
The outlaws, shy and gray like moss,
still in their dreams have the blood of fratricide
on their hands. Autumnal hunters following the tracks
of faithful barriers that bay with frost-clear voices?
Everyone and no one. We make the path together,
you too some windy day, when
it is early or else late on earth:
we write the paths, and the paths remain.
The paths are wiser than we are,
they know everything we'd like to know.

Martin Heidegger

The Pathway

(1947–1948)

translated by Thomas F. O'Meara, O.P.

It runs through the park gate and out towards Ehnried. The old linden trees in the castle garden gaze after it from behind the wall, whether at Easter when the path shines bright between growing crops and waking meadows, or at Christmas when it disappears in snowdrifts behind the nearest hill. At the wayside crucifix it turns off towards the woods. Along its edge it greets a tall oak beneath which stands a roughly hewn bench.

On the bench there occasionally lay one or another of the great thinkers' writings which youthful clumsiness was trying to decipher. When the puzzles crowded into each other and there seemed no way out, the pathway was a help. It quietly escorts one's steps along the winding trail through the expanse of untilled land.

Time and again when my thinking is caught in these same writings or in my own attempts, I go back to the trail traced by the pathway through the fields. It remains just as ready for the thinker's steps as for those of the farmer who goes out to mow in the early morning.

More frequently through the years, the oak by the wayside carries me off to memories of childhood games and early choices. When deep in the forest an oak would occasionally fall under the axe's blow, my father would immediately go looking throughout the woods and sunny clearings for the cord allotted him for his workshop. There he labored thoughtfully during pauses from his job of keeping the tower clock and the bells, both of which maintain their own relation to time and temporality.

From the bark of the oak tree little boys carved their boats which, fitted with rowers' benches and tillers, floated in Metten Brook or in the school fountain. On these journeys of play you could still easily get to your destination and return home again. The dream-element in such voyages remained held in a then hardly perceptible luster which lay over everything. The area of these journeys was circumscribed by the hand and eye of my mother. It was as if her unspoken care watched over everything. Those play voyages still knew nothing of wanderings when all shores would be left behind. Meanwhile, the hardness and scent of the oakwood began to speak more clearly of the slowness and constancy with which the tree grew. The oaktree itself spoke: only in such growth is there grounded what lasts and fructifies; to grow means to open oneself up to the expanse of heaven and at the same time to sink roots into the darkness of earth; everything genuine thrives only if it is, in right measure, both ready for the appeal of highest heaven and preserved in the protection of sustaining earth.

Again and again the oaktree says this to the pathway which passes by sure of its course. The pathway gathers in whatever has its Being around it; to all who pass this way it gives what is theirs. The same fields and meadows, ever changing but ever near, accompany the pathway through each season. Whether the Alps above the forests are sinking into twilight, or a lark is climbing into the summer morning where the pathway winds over the rolling hill, or the eastwind is blowing up a storm out of the region where mother's home village lies; whether, as night draws near, a woodsman drags his bundle of brushwood to the hearth, or a harvesting wagon sways homeward in the pathway's tracks, or children are gathering the first primroses at the meadow's edge, or the fog is pushing its gloomy burden over the fields for days on end—always and everywhere the call [*Zuspruch*][1] of the pathway is the same:

The simple preserves the enigma of what abides and is great. It comes to men suddenly but then requires a long time to mature. It conceals its blessings in the modesty of what is always the same. The wide expanse of everything that grows and abides along the pathway is what bestows world. In what its language does not say, there— says Eckhardt, old master of letter and life—God is truly God.

But the call of the pathway speaks only as long as there are men, born in its atmosphere, who can hear it. They are servants of their origin, not slaves of machination. Man's attempts to bring order to the world by his plans will remain futile as long as he is not ordered to the call of the pathway. The danger looms that men today cannot

---

1. The German *Zuspruch* can mean address, appeal, etc. The choice of "call" is as much an interpretation as a translation. The message, appeal, or address which the pathway (Greek, *he hodos*) sends to man is a summons, hence a call, into his essential self-absence.

hear its language. The only thing they hear is the noise of the media, which they almost take for the voice of God. So man becomes disoriented and loses his way. To the disoriented, the simple seems monotonous. The monotonous brings weariness, and the weary and bored find only what is uniform. The simple has fled. Its quiet power is exhausted.

Certainly the company of those who still recognize the simple as their hard-earned possession is quickly diminishing. But everywhere these few will be the ones who abide. Through the gentle force of the pathway they will one day have the strength to outlast the gigantic energies of atomic power, which human calculation has artificed for itself and made into fetters of its own action.

The call of the pathway awakens a sense which loves the free and open and, at the propitious place, leaps over sadness and into final serenity. This serenity resists the senselessness of merely working, which, when done for itself, promotes only emptiness.

In the pathway's seasonally changing breeze thrives this wise serenity whose mien often seems melancholy. This serene wisdom is at once "playful and sad, ironic and shy."[2] Someone who doesn't have it already can never acquire it. Those who have it get it from the pathway. Along its trail the winter storm encounters the harvest day, the lively excitement of spring meets the peaceful dying of autumn, the child's game and the elder's wisdom catch each other's eye. And all is serene in a singular harmony whose echo is silently carried here and there by the pathway.

Such wise serenity is a gateway to the eternal. Its door turns on hinges once forged by a skilled smith out of the enigmas of human existence.

From Ehnried the way turns back towards the park gate. Its narrow ribbon rises over the last hill and runs through some low ground until it reaches the town wall. It shines dimly in the starlight. There, behind the castle, rises the tower of St. Martin's Church. Slowly, almost hesitantly, eleven strokes of the hour sound in the night. The old bell, on whose ropes boys' hands were rubbed hot, shudders under the

---

2. *Das "Kuinzige"*: This phrase in Upper Swabian dialect is still in use in some areas. It is a dialect form for *kein nützend*, "not useful." From its originally negative tone it developed a positive meaning allied to "serene, playful." Heidegger paraphrases: "A serene melancholy which says what it knows with veiled expressions." (T.F.O'M.)

blows of the hammer of Time, whose dark-droll face no one forgets.

With the last stroke the stillness becomes yet more still. It reaches out even to those who were sacrificed before their time in two world wars. The simple has become simpler. The ever-same astonishes and liberates. The call of the pathway is now quite clear. Is it the soul speaking? or the world? or God?

Everything speaks of renunciation unto the same. Renunciation does not take away, it gives. It bestows the inexhaustible power of the simple. The call makes us at home in the arrival of a distant origin.

David Lloyd

"In a grey dawn . . . "

In a grey dawn awakening and maybe this is
The famous pass. Pitching high we are sung through yet
In a minor key and play it over and again. Dub dawn
And the mountains slope downwards cut off by the frames
The tumbling light brims over snagged in the brakes:
It's the old story deep recollection sneaks in

A streaky slick with the glimmer of boiled-out ink
Trails back and we call it anxious hunger. The break
Is here if ever, too true we all want to be
Rounded, but if you don't attend that break takes on
A morphic voice, like to the lark at break of day
Aching for the new moon and to be of the cusp.

On the rim of their voice you step up, hungering
For what slips between the doubles. Utopic dreams
Dissolve you, to the figures taking untold paths
Where you are powerless and would delay daylight
Under the fraying rains. Step back, her eye gives back
The distance where it detaches and fans away.

David Lloyd

"And as it pares off . . ."

And as it pares off it's with the reserved sound
Of the fabric shearing, a remote must-spoor
On the brink of the foregone. Take it from the draught
In passing, it is as if they slip into place
Where the misleaders thrashed out some kind of clearing:
The unheard-of tries for the rear of the sunlight

Set on the way from off a faulted track. All changed—
By mere citation—we hesitate on the step
Of what we were. Is it in their words? to bring us
To this pass, and southwards, the shimmer of delay
Withdrawing. That which will not meet us saps our strength,
Slipping unguarded into the enemy's habits.

Listen, it is the bulk of the world cascading
Over the selvedge in a confusion of light
And plunge. Though to rearwards is held out, the way is
Between, where the figures wedded in shadowbands
Lift apart in a moment of parting in which
The ground unsettles underneath the detachment.

David Lloyd

Medium

That is your own voice, insisting
on the playback. The figure
of the woman crosses between you
and the picture, shifting the still life.
But it's as she approaches at night,
unfamiliar and holding your heart in hand,
that's how it starts, only as a car
coughs off again from a stall. The firm curve
of the flyover tears back into the mist,
filling the gap where there wasn't any.
At first it's an outline and then
you're on it, the projection almost
the track retained. And if the rear screen
stars now with light flawed rain, it's an image
of violence we hold up, patient and
evasive, like when we told the old lady,
'we can as easily fall and break our necks'.
The suspension is deathly, reading the cards
on the long distance journey, long as you like.
                         There you find the gap
in your life, death or the not having known it,
and hang fire on whether it's what you
feel you need or what you want, the
oblivious object of invidia picked off,
and yourself rounded. Quite little and
shaken, he made for the father's lap, who
fondled his shock, sustained by the radio
going into the afterlife with a strange voice.
If the cards suspend you, those voices are
always and a little ahead with their

restraining murmur. Like honey from out
the strong they get all over till she
does you earth damage or in a real mist
in Reuland, coughing from a seasoned throat,
you weigh up the composed indifference
of the ode against the speechless Roman death.
The poet is all what doesn't survive
selection, it pauses at the knots,
rubbing back up against the forward grain
of history, where evening your own
loose end leaves the world a technical break.
The odds rush in there in a starry fray
like sparks enamoured of the gap thrust through,
and the flesh grows patient. So the quiet
and unexpected intimation of your death
steps between you and the familiar screen
as the voice you refused to admit
played back, or the words that were
for others only, engaged, say, mortal.
You take her up so, and with her
you take death on into your fort.

Sven Birkerts

Place: A Fragment

I was in the 1st grade before my parents finally found the house that they wanted to buy and our family moved. The "neighborhood" — though I don't think I ever called it that — was still largely undeveloped, with houses far apart and empty fields and wooded lots on all sides. Less than a mile away, to the north, there was a large, fenced-in (and, hence, perpetually mysterious) tract known as "Cousins Farm," with endless acres of pine forest, a long weedy pond full of bluegills and turtles, open hillsides that were sometimes dotted with grazing cows — at other times they were perplexingly bare! — and a dark, abandoned cabin that looked down over the far side of the pond. During the summers and after school we were always calling over the shoulder that we were "going over to Cousins . . . " We scuttled through the barbed-wire like thieves, hunkered low as we crossed the open field, and exhaled with relief as soon as we got over the planks at the edge of the pond. In the safe murk of the pines, we explored, built forts, conducted important meetings. One ear was always cocked for a rustle or a cracking branch: much of the thrill of being at Cousins had to do with its illegality: WARNING — NO TRESPASSING.

My parents still live in that house, and I go back to the neighborhood several times a year. The contour of the land is the same, but suburban scurf has obscured everything else. Cousins Farm — it disappeared overnight — is now a pricy development boasting its own 18-hole golf course. The desecration of the neighborhood had been going on all along — a house here, another there — but we (my friends and I) didn't much mind it. Indeed, a good deal of our activity centered on those construction sites. We looted them for boards and nails; we roamed through half-finished interiors, making little fires, scratching our names, peeing (Dylan Thomas was right: young boys are like dogs!) . . . There were still woods, fields, and swamps everywhere. It only dawned on us later that the changes were permanent, and by that time we were beginning to develop other interests.

A quick, time-lapse account. It's logically sound — that *is* what happened — but it bears not the slightest relation to the experience of childhood. But then, nothing I say out of the perspective of retrospect touches it. My words sooner refute than encompass that earlier world. No matter what plea or adjustment I make, I cannot catch hold of the peculiar magic of those places. It is less that *they* are gone than that *I* am. No effort of will can restore to me that perception, that view of the horizon not yet tainted by futurity — it runs me through sometimes, but I cannot summon it.

And yet everything I would say about place depends on it, and everything I search for in myself involves some deep fantasy of its restoration. My best, truest — I cannot define my terms — self is vitally connected to a few square miles of land. I call up images of it in reverie, or when I want to calm myself into sleep — or sometimes while making love. And when I go home to visit I behave as if it had never existed.

I had a happy childhood. That's what I say now. Back then it was not one thing or another, just a way things had of happening, a natural and unquestioned waking up and going about the daily business. I see now that I was full to the brim, with nothing lacking; that space and time were not yet separable concepts, scarcely concepts at all. "Weren't you ever bored?" Dear God, I was in an ecstasy of boredom! I was so bored that time would back up on itself and start flowing in a new direction. And yet it wasn't like the trivial boredom that afflicts me now. It was a dream, a plenitude. The whole of my childhood was inoculated with it. Boredom: mother of absorption. Afternoons that turned honey-thick, chasing me out of my room and into the fields, along trails, down into the oozy reeds of the swamp. Such impenetrable silence, such a stupor — over and over it forced me out of myself. Combustions of fantasy, riotous private ritual. And then the inevitable crash. I would suddenly be slammed back against my own boundaries. I would stare at the husk, the tree that was just a tree, no longer a secret look-out post . . . No escape, no place to go. The soldering heat of late summer.

I don't know, now, if I actually felt places as animate, or if I have imposed that as a false memory. Surely I knew that some spots were haunted and others beneficent. But was there anything more? Nowadays, I often catch myself regarding some particular landscape as if it were possessed of passive sentience. Have I become more spiritually attuned? Or is it simply that landscape itself has become an emblem of the timeless perception of childhood? When, as sometimes happens, I feel as though I'm on the brink of touching something — is it that? Could it be that the living otherness I sense is nothing more than the self that I had to bury?

Thomas Paladino

Spoken Charm For Our Current Ignorance

You must call the stone by name
crying loudly: "Rock Untunjambili
open, that I may enter."

Your last of three wishes may fail.
Then the search for a cause will begin
by chastizing the chant whose rhythm is difficult.
Men will go home and beat their wives;
women will beg to sacrifice their birthright.
Only a bird's blade-like tongue will answer.

But empty of all contest, all ridicule,
one may return alone at night
to answer deafness by rubbing the stone.

Thomas Paladino

The Theory of Omens

The Great Mother spreads her ass
and the lords of the valley bow.

Thomas Paladino

In The Likeness

Earth,
our stemless globe of fruit,
rolling on without thought,
memory, dream or desire.

Yes. For once, say it out loud.
Don't be embarrassed. Say it:

O labia that culls through space
the stubborn world of matter
my compliments to the wheel!

Geoffrey Young

Meander Walk

The best walks are walks alone. Best time to walk through Western Massachusetts woodland is mid to late April while you can feel spring stirring but you won't be impeded by its flowering profusion. On a ridge trail of limestone shelf.

Last year's undergrowth flat pressed to the ground, in grays and browns, short weeks after the blanket snows of late March. You can see *through* the forest, see the land forming the shape of your walk, you can leave the trail and wander. There's something about a trail this time of year makes you want to leave it anyway, to follow your nose. To picture a shady rock.

Indeed, your very presence here is a function of spring, your eagerness equal to the tiny snaps, crackles and pops the forest floor makes as it dries, contracts, prepares to rise as crook-necked ferns.

You straddle a puddle, looking up at scatter, the wrack, at the lines and shapes made by windblown branches, last fall's matted leaves gathered in hollows, clots of organic debris in a fallen tree's exposed roots. Dead tendrils of fern splayed flat, sponge moss on exposed rock, you touch it, a few ounces, or quarts, or gallons of melted snow reflecting an even gray sky.

Your ears are as much your guide as your eyes are, where the sound is diffuse, mute, unequally mixed in air. Up, over, around, you pick your way to a vantage from which you can see moss and lichen blend greens in an opening. Warmer now, and by chance, an infrequent tiny flower. A snowdrop or purple heartbeat. You visit each.

There is no one talking to you but what you sense, you are neither leading nor following someone, you're balanced on an elm stump, leaping over a rotting birch. Fenceless, each space slides perfectly into the next, your direction mapped by what attracts you. A pile of rocks, for example, half legible field stones heaped, means previous inhabitation. You try and imagine these spaces cleared, almost see black and white cows grazing here, or a field of corn, a field of timothy and clover.

Deer droppings everywhere. Occasional spoor of fox. Walking, but not steadily, not *going* somewhere, exactly, following the lay of the land past marked trees, big crosses painted blue on mature pines — abandoned plans? Stoop to lift thick matted grass with gloved fingers, find bedrock two inches beneath, no soil at all, the grass a woven rug not penetrating the rock. Here.

Maple branch cracks in half underfoot, dowsy to the core. All this potential firewood rotting back into the ground, feeding as it fades the soil from which yet another generation of trees and shrubs is stirring, is striving, jockeying for nutrients in tangled root webs underground.

Nature may be indifferent to us, but it is nothing less than ambitious for itself, obeying rules that define us as well, no matter how much we think ourselves separate. We are transitional characters. Each walking space is nursery, combat zone, and cemetery alike. Up close, species by species, individual sapling by lichen by worm, an efficient and highly detailed conversion is going on at every level, the rock below holding all this humorless self-possession in relation.

These little Berkshire hills, gray rounded limestone ancient nubbins once huge and the ice not due back for 90,000 years. Stop and breathe, cool air scented with pine and unfrozen mud. Walking is a percolation. For no reason, near a chaos of sprawled birch branches, near a bark-peeling upended trunk lodged in the crotch of a white pine bough, you think of Kerouac's description in *Tristessa* of walking through a Mexico City rainstorm, minting impressions. Then of St. Augustine's description of his mother's faith, her death and funeral. Tiny pinpoints of light poke through leaden sky, momentarily lighting a seam of quartz. You make a point of walking around not through a never-harvested, never-sold forest of now tall and ugly light-shielding Christmas trees twenty years old.

Come upon a stream that is a spring bubbling up from under a jutting boulder, water so cold it hurts the hand that cups it. Compelled to an edge, that in summer would be a screen of leaves, you view a valley. You sit on a treetrunk fallen into the form of a bench, its bark long since fallen off, listening to a slight breeze chill. Nearby, charred on one side, a tree blasted by lightning and violently toppled, its trunk's splintered spikes in air still blonde.

Birds flit behind branches of hemlock, protected. But for one deer surprised in a dark forest, bounding away and followed into a field of thorny bushes, you have seen no mammal, other than yourself, half alien, half predator of unpatterned sensation. It is time to turn back, knowing that to get lost is but to be delayed. And that it could happen to you. Is that why you laugh? No one hears you. Your eye works differently on the way back. Now memory edits choice, little pangs of anxiety are registered in the unfamiliar look of certain spaces you approach.

No shortcut that isn't also a potential drifting off course. No sunlight, no pieces of red wool. Until, at last, after some misgivings and considerable distance, through a welter of tangled branches and uneven ground, you spot a fragment of a house painted white, and you know.

Thomas Frick

Down in the Place: Notes from Münster

Michelle Ebersohl of Pfafenhofen came by early one Saturday to pick us up in her Citroën *deux chevaux.* It was a breezy, sparkling day in Alsace, and she was taking us on a hiking trip near Münster, the town where, growing up, she'd spent summers with her parents. Münster, in the Vosge Mountains of Eastern France, is where Münster cheese originated; suffice it to say that what Americans know as "Münster cheese" bears, if not absolutely no, then only the most minimal relation to the original product. When we bought our nine-inch wheel of it from a small table in the Münster market square, we were asked when we planned to eat it—today, tomorrow, the next day?—and were given a riper cheese, ready for our picnic that afternoon. I bought five nice tomatoes, and Michelle wanted to get some bread from a particular bakery she remembered. She wasn't sure exactly where it was, and after looking down two or three side streets, she turned back towards the market and quickened her steps. "Oh, I am sure we will find it down in the place."

Down in the place! Michelle speaks fluent German, Alsatian, French, and English, the last with a charming musical facility, though occasionally an idiom trips her. In this case, however, I suddenly saw that the misusage was not hers, but ours—that of our land, and thence of our language. Down in the place—it's a perfectly sensible translation of the French *dans la place. Place de Broglie, Place Gutenberg, Place Kleber*—Strasbourg, like all French cities, is dotted with these sites, each a *place.* The smallest village has one; they don't have to have names. In German, *platz;* in Spanish, *plaza;* in Italian, *piazza;* the languages are in accord on this form of life. The only legitimate English translation would be "place;" yet we are placeless in this sense. Undefined common public spaces, each an axis of all forms of public human interaction, space with a historical density great enough to resist encroachment—this hardly exists in the United States, so we have no word for it. Instead we import a word, "plaza" perhaps, to refer to engineered interstices, deserted and trash-ridden, within an "environment" built on an increasingly non-human scale.

As we began our ascent, Michelle confided to me that these hills made her feel a little sad, since she had climbed them often with her former boyfriend. "But it's okay, once we get up, it is good, I like to hike . . . "

Later as we sat eating our lunch of tomatoes, bread, Münster, and Orangina, sheltered by trees and boulders halfway up a valley, listening to cows and watching the sky move, the cloud-shadows play variously across the rocky valley sides, I had a vision of our three-dimensional earthly orb as a tiny spinning shuttle in an immense gyroscopic web — vast armatures of color transcending earthly spectra, astronomical filaments of light. This loom in which our planet is imbedded is no mere machine, is a living structure, or a frame for the operations and movements of many concerned beings, in and out, "up and down," beings always involved in our affairs, whose concern is increasing as the speed of time, the swift cloud-shadows racing over the valley. This is the whole, of which our planet, and our awareness of it, is only part. Thus, here, ("this tiny here" as Fred Brown wrote) we all are "down in the place" of Earth, down in the place, of space, of time.

David Boardman

Written on the Rocks

Buildings and monuments
made of granite stand impermeable;
the cliffs stand solid in the gorge.
Timber covers the mountains above

the granite and basalt rock,
rugged grandeur immense
for miles of silence
among mossy trees and stone.

Water falls from the top
of the massive gorge
and the old stone bridges
cross the creeks.

Along the old scenic highway
gates open to the wilderness
where one can find himself
standing as one alone

in a forest above noise,
standing with wind,
hot August sun
and trees telling the way.

Grave markers made of granite
mark the past of people who
died. The rock still stands
unchanged. The people die,

but their names are written
on the rocks like Indian
petroglyphs in the obsidian
and basalt rock.

In the desert and woods
graveyards are present,
marking the past, who
dies and the date.

Wild iris grows around
the old desert graveyard.
People died young back then,
dying much earlier than today.

Times were hard.
Death is a frequent thing
and is all over the valleys,
mountains and desert, is
written in the rocks.

David Boardman

Rock and Wind

I was at one with rock and wind.
The surly wind whipped wisps
around the steady rocks.
Flagging, it flew around the trees.

The stealthy water moved in swirls
as gray dark and light
streaked across its painted mirror.
The face of the deep-rooted gorge
reflected its rugged beauty.

The scarred edges outlined the sky
with folded hills tucked and wrapped,
barren billowing hills rolling
stretching lofty away around the water,
leaving its giant face

on the big gray waters of river
with bridges and tunnels
winding through and around
the steep massive canyon.
Loaves of broad brown hills

near the steel gray Columbia,
wind whinnying up the hills
and across the stalky fields
where I lay tired and lonely,
as one with rock and wind.

Friedrich Hölderlin

(But when the gods . . .)

translated by Richard Sieburth

But when the gods have done
Building, silence comes over
The earth, and the mountains
Stand finely shaped, their features
Traced. For as the Thunderer
Contended with his daughter,
They were struck by
The god's trembling ray,
And fragrance descends
As the uproar wanes.
Where it lies within, soothes, here
And there   the fire.
For the Thunderer showers
Forth joy and would have
Almost forgotten heaven
In his wrath, had not
Wisdom given him warning.
But now even poor places
Are in flower.
And will rise
Majestic.
Mountain overhangs   lake,
Warm   deep   but breezes cool
Islands and peninsulas,
Grottoes for praying,

A sparkling shield,
And quick, as roses

Reprinted by permission of Princeton University Press from
Hymns and Fragments by Friedrich Hölderlin.

                              or else creates

Other ways,
But the sprouting of
                    rank envious
Weeds, deceptive as they shoot
Up quick and uncouth,
For the Creator has tricks
They do not understand. It grasps
And spreads with too much fury. And like fire
Consuming houses, lashes
Out, uncaring, and spares
No space and covers paths,
Seething everywhere, a smoldering cloud
                         wilderness without end.
Seeking to pass for something
Godly. But Error reels eyeless
Through the garden, dreadful,
Inhospitable, since no man
With clean hands can
Find exit. He proceeds, driven
Like a beast in search of
Necessities. Though with his arms
And premonitions, a man may reach
The goal. For where
The gods require fences or markers
To indicate their path,
Or need a pool to bathe,
The hearts of men
Beat like fire.

But the Father had others
By his side.
For above the Alps
Where poets must rely
Upon the eagle, lest their angry
Interpretations make mere private sense,
And living above the flight
Of birds, around the throne
Of the Lord of Joy

From whom they conceal
The abyss, these, the prophetic ones,
Lie above the gaze of men
Like yellow fire, in torn
Times, envied by those in love
With fear, the shades of hell,

But they were driven,
A pure fate
Opening   from
The sacred tables of the earth
Hercules the Purifier
Who remains undefiled to this day
With the Lord, and the breath-bearing
Dioscuri climb up and down
Inaccessible stairs as the mountains
Retreat from the heavenly fortress
At night, and gone
The times
Of Pythagoras.

Philoctetes lives in memory.

They go to the Father's aid
For they desire rest. But when
The useless doings of the earth
Provoke them and from the gods
Are taken
                senses, they then come
Burning

These without breath

For thoughtful God
Detests
Untimely growth

Friedrich Hölderlin

The Nearest the Best

translated by Richard Sieburth

the windows of heaven are open,
The spirit of night is on the loose,
Who takes the sky by storm and has confounded
Our land with a babble of tongues, and
Stirred up rubble
To this very day.
But my wishes will be realized
When

Thus like starlings
With screams of joy, when above Gascogne, regions of countless
　　gardens,
When fountains, where olives grow
On lovely foreign soil, when trees
By grassy paths
Unaware in the wild
Are stung by the sun,
And earth's heart
Opens, where rivers
From the burning plain
Flow around hills
Of oak, where
Sundays, amid dancing,
Thresholds offer welcome and
Blossoms wreathe the quiet procession of streets.
They sense their native land,
When the silver waters trickle
From pale yellow rock
And the holiness of green is revealed
On the moist meadows of the Charento,

Cultivating keen senses.   but when
The breeze carves its way
And the sharp northeasterly
Quickens their eyes, they fly up,
And at every corner
Lovelier things draw into their sight,
For they cleave to what is nearest,
And see the sacred forests and the flame of growth
In fragrant flower and the distant choirs of clouds breathe in
The breath of songs. Recognition
Is human. But the gods
Have this in them too, and observe the hours
At dawn and birds at dusk. So this
Also pertains to the gods. Well, fine. There was a secret
Time when by nature I would have said
They were coming to Germany. But now, since the earth
Is like the sea, and the nations, like men who cannot
Cross to each other's coasts, squabble
Among themselves, I speak as follows. To the west, well-forged,
The mountains curve down from the uplands where woods on
   high meadows
Overlook the Bavarian plain. For the range
Reaches far, stretching beyond Amberg and
The Franconian hills. This is well known. Not for nothing
Did someone curve the range away from the mountains
Of youth and face it
Homewards. To him the Alps are a wilderness and
The mountains that sever valleys, strung lengthwise
Across the earth. But there

          and trees rejoice and rustle over the peaked
Shelter. What is in place is good. But one thing
We grapple with. It hangs on, nearly depriving us of the holy spirit.
Barbarians also live where the sun and moon
Reign alone. But God sustains us, if indeed there be one, would that
· He change my fatherland around.

Now, to move on. The spirit was
The horse's flesh. But at Ilion
Was also the light of eagles. But in the middle

The Nearest the Best / 71

The heaven of songs. But next to this,
Angry old men, on the shore of judgment,
All three of which ours.

George Steiner

Cairns

Walking

We forget that the preponderance of Western thought, motions
of spirit (Dante's phrase), acts of feeling and inward recognition arose
walking. That reflection and imagination and the current of silent
speech that generates, cradles, transmutes the impulses of the sub-
conscious, were organized by the pulse and pace of walking. And that
the quality of such thought and sensibility is immediately shot through
by the particular economy of bodily forces which walking entails. That
the relations of perception between muscle and distance, between eye
and terrain, between skin and weather, experienced by a walker are
enveloping and distinctive. We forget what space and time signified,
felt, "tasted" like to one who reckoned the map and the hour in terms
of walking from point to point, from town to town, across borders.
(Kant was, reputedly, a metronomically exact walker; how does this
constancy relate to his categorical determinants of space and time?)
A walked world is radically different from one traveled over in a train,
automobile, or airplane. In what ways is the present dialectic of poli-
tical-ethnic ecumenism and the equally strong counterforce of paro-
chialism a direct reflection of the compressions of climate and land-
mass, of time and physical setting that come of flying? Only the eccentric or archeologist of feeling now knows what it is to walk the
bounds of reality, to restore to native logic the capacities of the body
and the dimensions of the environment.

This logic was inherent in the romantic movement. Wordsworth
walks from Calais to the St. Gothard and back. Coleridge regards twenty miles over mountainous and boggy terrain as average. Hölderlin,
not a strong man, walks from the Rhineland to Bordeaux and back

Reprinted by permission of author from *The Mountain Spirit,*
eds: Michael Tobias and Harold Drasdo © Overlook Press 1979

via Paris. Hebbel walks the length of Germany. (Byron's clubfoot does not prevent him from forays into the Alps, but he is essentially a rider, and his longer poems are instinct with a rider's motion and modulations of cadence.) The revolutionary and Napoleonic wars transform men of a perfectly ordinary physique into prodigious walkers. Thus Stendhal *walks* to Moscow and back in 1812, and we cannot begin to gauge the aesthetics of energy in *The Charterhouse of Parma* or *The Red and the Black* without reflecting on what this means. To put it abruptly: the two great poles of ego and nature, of personal consciousness and felt world, which define romanticism and of which modernism is the direct heir, were determined by, sprang from, walking. Rousseau knew this. He articulated the new subjectivism around a gamut of walks—the whole way from the enormous cross-country marches of the young man to the "promenades" of the old. We have forgotten.

Associations

When a Sunday skirter of hills and funicular tiger like myself tries to image, to put into words, his sense of the mountains, clichés and spurious profundities cascade. The slow movement of Mahler's Fifth Symphony and the ascendant arcs in Bruckner's Eighth. The total but hammering stillness of the air in a high dingle or cwm. The stone smell, like metal, just above the tree line. The archetypal rummage of symbols—paternalistic, sexual, death-laden—which legend, psychoanalysis, Jungian animism, and nineteenth-century painting have attached to high peaks, to tenebrous valleys, to crevasses, and to what Hölderlin called the *belle Nacht*, the "luminous, lambent night" of spindrift and vapor in an alpine cirque. Even the very great artists and poets overstate or become formulaic. Coleridge's, Shelley's, Byron's versions of the Mont Blanc group or Jungfrau massif are finally pompous and indistinct. Nietzsche's Engadin can overdramatize and bully (it is in the strenuous yet marvelously elastic *gait* of his later philosophic writings, writings composed during walks around Sils, that the mountain experience is best translated). Hills are more manageable: Wordsworth's "Prelude" is matchless on Skiddaw and Helvellyn, as are Keats's letters. Cézanne's successive versions of the Mont St. Victoire are "of the hills hilly," internalizing to the touch and, with uncanny exactitude, the feel of rock and scree and light. Auden's *Ascent of F6* is almost embarrassing, but he is confident on the Northumberland fells and amid the dark, humped lava hills of Iceland.

The thing is terribly difficult to do well. D. H. Lawrence is frenetic and banal on the Bavarian alps but superb when he evokes the Rockies and the brooding weight of the Mexican *cordillera*. Ramuz is fine when he treats the mountains as the furnishings of work for those who live among them. Broch's *Bergroman* is not free of vaporous solemnities, but no one has come closer to pinning down in words the play of light and weather, of sound and scent around the snow crests and rock walls of the Tyrolian alps (the *Nordkette* above the luminous cut of the Inn valley). And there is a perfect poem by I. A. Richards about leaping a crevasse in the dark — which is, to that great Platonist-mountaineer, "the only way to live."

But for the armchair-scrambler, his muscles burning, his breath steamy with doubt over the whole mousey venture — "can I reach that lowest, almost hotel-like refuge," "can I puff to the top of the ski-lift?" — the problem is the opposite. To keep lofty overtones at bay, to keep the great dark chords from sounding around his wobbly knees. To *see* what is *there* (through the sweat on his glasses). To know ridicule, and not mind too much.

Sea and Mountain

Wanted: A contrastive political theory of both. Already the ancient Greeks felt the issue to be a vital and confusing one. The empirical-symbolical readings of the sea are those of "openness," "freedom," "sophistication." The man who dwells near and travels across open water is, almost by definition, a free man, a tolerant perceiver of the world's diversities, a spirit whose relationship to nature is at once wary and intellectually inventive. By contrast, the mountaineer is enclosed, prone to xenophobia and archaic imaginings. His comportment has in it strong traces of a primal, almost animal state of solitude and territoriality. Of necessity, he spends a good part of his existence in shadow or raw cold. The inhuman dimensions of the mountains both exalt and dwarf his individuality. The avalanche and the rock fall lie in ambush. He speaks in dialect. He stands, often in precarious verticality, at the cleft or narrows, not in the open agora. His horizon is a wall, where the sea is a gate flung open by the light. Yet, note the antique observers, it is frequently the mountaineer who is most jealous of his freedom, and the harbor man who is servile. It is the Thracian, it is the aboriginal of the Caucasus who will not be subdued, where the Minoan or the Syracusan bends to the despot.

The paradox persists in later "geopolitical" speculations. To

Milton, to the romantics, to the political exiles of the nineteenth and twentieth centuries, Switzerland incarnates liberty and the Rousseauist dream of plebiscitary government. At the very same time, the poetics and metaphysics of elitist thought, from de Maistre to Nietzsche and Heidegger, are closely knit to the actual or allegoric presence of high mountains. The Bavarian and Tyrolean alps, the Eiger, the needles of the Dolomites play a notorious role in the fantasy lives, in the *rites of passage*, of the National Socialist and Fascist movements (Riefenstahl's allegorization of the assaults on the Eiger remains a formidable witness).

This equivocation is considered, most deeply, in *The Magic Mountain*. Starting with its famous first sentence, the whole novel turns on the pendulum motion between the North Sea coast and the ice cones above Davos. Twice, the structure of narrative and of meaning is that of ascent, from the *Flachland* to the summits, twice it is that of descent into the world of humane commitment which is also that of death. In the heart of the pattern stands the snowstorm, the literal white-out in which Hans Castorp's soul is driven to the roots of its being and solicited by the inhuman order of elemental agencies. In the political dialectic which is the axis of the book, the mobile sea argues against the mountain. Thomas Mann does not choose explicitly. He is as ambiguously at home in the Hanseatic ports and marine Venice as in the Berner Oberland. But he knows that the polarity is fundamental, that it classifies the sensibilities and the utopias of Western culture since the pre-Socratics. Norway is the puzzler: the one landscape where great towers of rock and snow anchor directly in a racing sea. Ibsen's *Brand* is driven by this crazy conjunction.

Marginal

In those small autobiographical notices one is asked for, I list music, chess, and mountain walking as "recreations." The word should be: "obsessions," "compulsions," uttermost desiderata. Not that I have anything to contribute, actively. The only musical instruments I play are, as the undergraduate jibe has it, high fidelity and low fidelity. In chess I am a desperate wood pusher, a Knight-to-Rook-4 fugitive because opening theory leaves me hamstrung. And my mountain walking is, increasingly, that of a mildly obese turtle, breathing loudly, triggering derisive miniature avalanches from underpebbles, and straining to keep my balance on the most domestic of slopes. Nevertheless, the three things are indispensable to me. And somehow, I know that there are relations between them. Not by vague, archetypal association. But somewhere in an intensely crucial, deep-buried synapse where the fields of force, of energized space in the musical sequence and on the chessboard meet with the play of sinew and distance that is climbing. Where the charged silences between bars congrue, somehow, with those that give to a chess game its stifled violence, and can, in turn, be matched with the mountain whorls of quiet (the words get it wrong, unavoidably). And there are precise spots, one in a valley upward from Aosta and under the Monte Rosa glacier, where the immaterial concreteness of music, the alternate rush and repose of chess, and the fact of the mountains come together, in a fusion that is, to me, more compact with meaning than any other experience. I *know* this to be so, in the skin of my being. I cannot articulate or prove it.

Having written (inadequately) about music and chess, I construe these cairns. In the margin. To thank.

Novalis

from The Notebooks

translated by Thomas Frick

Spirit is active, now here, now there. When will Spirit be active all over? When will mankind as a whole begin to *consider*?

Nature is pure pastness, freedom abandoned. Thus nature is everywhere the ground on which history grows, season after season.

Daytime is the consciousness of a planet. The sun, like a god, inspires the center. One planet after another closes one eye for a longer or shorter period, and with cool sleep refreshes itself for new contemplation. As man is like the sun, so his senses are like the planets.

If God can become man, he can also become element, stone, plant, animal. Perhaps there is a continual Redemption in nature.

Has the increase in cultivation produced changes in Nature? Was Nature always obedient to laws, and will she remain so? Has Nature not essentially changed with the progress of culture?

Space is a precipitate of time. Every body is a completed impulse. An individual in space is a body. An individual in time is a soul. All actual commencement is secondary momentum.

Genuine philosophy is communion with a dearly loved world. One follows the sun, and tears oneself from the place which, owing to the revolution of the planet, will be plunged into frigid night and mist. Death is the philosophical act within everyone.

Every line is the axis of a world.

Wonders alternate with the natural. They mutually limit each other and form a harmonious whole.

If the world is a tree, then we are the blossoms.

The specific gravity of the earth is almost the same as that of the diamond. Possibly the core of the earth is a diamond.

When you see a giant, check the angle of the sun. It might be the long shadow of a pigmy.

Philosophy is homesickness.

Mist rising from the water is prayer. Nature has allegories of her own.

Paradise was the ideal of earthly life, and the question of its whereabouts is not unimportant. It has been scattered all over the world, and has become unrecognizable. Its scattered traits must be collected, its skeleton filled in.

It is only because we are weak and self-conscious that we don't actualize the life of fairytales. Fairytales are dreams of the Home World, which is everywhere and nowhere. Our own higher powers, which shall one day carry out our wishes, are now merely Muses, which refresh us on the weary path with the charms of memory.

The sluggishness of our spirit oppresses us. But we can change our active life into fate. Everything seems to swamp us because we do not flow out. We are negative from choice. The more "positive" we become, the more "negative" the world, until there is no more negative. God wills gods.

Robin E. van Löben Sels

Wanting a Country for This Weather

See the slow rise of this watercolored morning:
how the light hangs in clefts;
how the high grass bends, early with light,
and the breathing fields flash in the ringing air.

Not that there was not night.
But hear: how sings the light

that this is our wish, blue with night and longing,
gentled by grass and greened to an early birth:
lit by the brimming hills, unconscionably fair,
that this be the homeland of our love's lost morning.

Richard Grossinger

from The Planet With Blue Skies

(unpublished manuscript, 1974-5)

A remembered dream emerges clearly out of a long unknown dream. I am on a plane, and we have been flying over the Atlantic. We have been in the air a long time. There is no sense of whether it is hours, days, or months, but the cumulative image is that we have entered totally new territory. We have passed beyond the curvature of the Earth.

We are approaching England, people seem to feel. It is near dawn. I look out of the plane and see a small irregular island in the sea. It looks less like an island than a late Renaissance map of an island, with all houses drawn in, little sheep and goats mixed in with topographical markers. The pilot says that we are going to land there because of a detour. We circle it again and again from the air, making a lower pass each time. It is clear that we do not need to adjust our trajectory so many times to make a landing. There must be some other problem. Each time we swoop over, the island is closer, the image of it intenser, the dawn further advanced. But the people on the island, the woman carrying the baskets, the shepherd and his goats, the men in the boathouses by the shore, on the edge of the forest, do not seem to be moving. Or they are moving so slowly that they look like photographs though the cumulative effect of the dawn is to bring them along through their activities. We are coming closer and closer to them, to their time. I feel that this is an illicit landing in every sense. We can't be here. We can't come here by plane, and yet that is what we are doing. I think of the Cranberry Islands, the Canaries; there is something about this island that has to do with them. It is older than everything we know. It is undisturbed. They do not see the plane. We can land and refuel at some unmanned service pump and they will not even know we have been there.

I long to be on the island, not only to be there but to be so part of it that its mystery is in me. Not as I see it from the plane but that those in the plane see *me*, and *I* am not even aware of its landing and departing. I am the darkness.

The houses are old and covered with moss and vines. They have grown in place like caves that are also trees. The land is map, is parchment, but a blue palpable sea rushes over it and fertilizes its brown aging pages. The people will live forever. This is not an island only. This is the lost hermetic text.

The Canaries are part of North America. The Cranberries are part of Europe. I see the bright white quartz crystals littered in Central Park, hidden away there like gems. I see them from the air. The park is in Asia, on an island off Japan. It is civilized without contact with the rest of civilization. Not one bird has visited, one seed washed ashore on derelict cargo. Just because we have planes does not mean we can intrude upon them.

We make one last swoop, very low, and at an angle of such precise variance from one hundred and eighty degrees, that I see over the island, I see further out to sea, there is another island, a bare rock, which is on no map, which is inhabited even more lushly and fantastically than this one, but to us seems no more than a rock in the waves, waves which have become black. At our angle it is impossible to tell whether the rock emerges from the sea or sits out beyond the Sun in space.

*　　　*　　　*

Seeing the Hyades with binoculars, looking into the actual snarl at location. The field changes. There is a dense innering of stars, and those that are visible from the Earth sea sit around them, the brain of the Bull, the bloody active Brain of the Bull. I follow it across the sky, through the cradle of Cassiopeia, into the Pleiades, clustered gems.

The names are as old to language as the stars are to sky. They are light. They are also obstruction. Their only message is what gets through. And gives with burning clarity the blackness of the rest. Because there are no other. Castor and Pollux. The faint Lynx.

They are the whole of our history. They are ceaselessly falling as snow falls. Nothing is falling, but electric charge, and that falls within the dark winter bark of the trees as well, and in this mind. For where matter is merged with an active principle, creation seems to begin. Our being here, the cold wind on my cheeks, lifting my hair and dropping it. This is why the design cannot be built by itself alone. This is why we stand in the night sky to see what the design is. This is why the brightness and sharpness and perspective of it all overwhelms me and forms in me a prayer. St. Anselm speaks his thanks to the outermost powers bringing his mind this far before he begins his famous proof of God.

There is no ideal world, there is only this one, the sky says. The fire on the hill becomes the Moon rising late, Canis tumbling as it climbs. Every part moving in touch with every other part because coherence subsumes the individual images. How in t'ai chi the striking arm goes back behind the ear, turning over, stepping out, sinking, and then rising. A fish leaps, to touch the frozen tip of ice.

*   *   *

The sun burns out the zodiac, crossing the blue winter sky. From the torso of Virgo on Maple Hill to the three stars of Aries over Plainfield Village. Behind that streaming daylight creation is, the fountain of creation, we wrote once on a golden dome. Have we forgotten? Have we forgotten so much we have forgotten it all? A law Newton barely salvaged, off the surface of the broken disc. Eternal time submerged in daily time. However faint Cancer and Pisces, they too, houses of the sun. So that planets must also be found there, wandering in Leo and the Beehive (in China, Exhalation of Piled-Up Corpses, 150 stars of 6th magnitude or less: the Cloudy One, in which they — they weren't astronomers — observed Mercury passing, June 9, 118). The sun washing out the rest for the better part of a thousand years. Or Dante: "I woke to find myself in a dark wood,/Where the right road was wholly lost and gone."

*   *   *

"See-saw, Marjorie Daw. Jackie will have a new master."

But the strangeness and obscurity is not just the old apartment in the city, and not just the fullness to me. Nor is it Hamlet's mill, that the sky is torn apart in a history that exceeds all but our best and most ancient books.

And yet I am tracking in back of that history, thru Vergil, Homer, along the 293 + stars of Eridanus, a meandering and faint stream from Orion to a southern Pacific sky. Not as stellar structure but crystal of mind and suspension, Hamal, Sharatan: the Ram. The stars of history that burned down the avenues of Mediaeval cities, when those cities were fields, and the merchants wandered between them, their coins blank, their parchment deeded in an Egypt long out of business, until Europe saw once again, off the horizon of Twelfth Century Asia, its forgotten face. And value became wheat and wool. As Hesiod sought boundary, in creation, of sea and sky.

Picking my way thru quadrants and kingdoms, Algol via Capella, downstream to Phecde and Dubhe, the Bear, his tail: Alioth, Mizar, Alkaid. And on the second March night Arcturus breathes over Maple Hill. How far we have come without coming any distance at all. Hoops on a barrel you might say, as night turns within night, as Indian stars break apart, littering the sky with an eagle, a snake, and three deer (North America only), a jaguar and a pig to the south. Hoops on a barrel, but I know better. I know that the images rush through nursery rhymes like trains, and their nonsense is the bare degree of shape left in constellations, as time itself, nonexistent, bears it away, through the transit of our known lives. Who were those merchants who bought back Europe from the East? No friends of mine, says Charlemagne, years too late. And the Romans never knew. They live in Rome to this day, unaware that the Dragon has fallen. Who were the Normans who visited the Plough? From whence the Minoans, bearing the hieroglyph for emmer wheat (the seed also?), and a night-demon named Lyl, later Lylyt? And who lived there before them, in villages, to receive it into a sky filled already with kings, an Earth sown with Mesolithic grain?

The sun passes through the outer door, and a broken transmission is dropped on us. Broken by those who would have us restore it. Through the kingdom pass the same beings who always passed, their roles gradually changing, bent and driven down, Draco with Thuban, once the Pole Star, once to which the Pyramids of Egypt pointed, I now see faintly against the North American mountains. Falls into a Crocodile, into language. The Dipper is broken and the Throne of the Five Emperors falls. We have lived too long, say those who are now dead. Sirius, bearing Egyptian summer, in Vermont winter, trails Procyon and Gomeisa, Canis Minor, if conjunct with Mercury, person dies of dog bite, or is it some other bite entirely, H.D.?, the dogs the Romans sacrificed in 238 B.C. to keep mildew from their fields, long before the Saxon councils and the fixed-star astrologers of the North.

An old man with a battered book, a druid, a rabbi, a dervish, a beggar: he says we pass through unbroken night. And I will lead you, he does not say. Not yet. Is still the origin. And origin, by measurements the Greeks took at the beginning, is destiny. As history writes itself in fire, light alone measures decay, its choking rate, where only the nova fires fade from the flank of Cassiopeia, where Kochab measures through Thuban the line of the top of the world, from which astral and royal power, because the seal is eternal, pours down night and day, despite the city-blown traceries of electrode cool. The bite still lingers, believe in it or not; the stars turn and shift, history to the northern forest frontier of Rome, while Rome like a candle burned off the Orient, the wood-priest holding a broken plough. Stone for stone against the opening of another day.

*   *   *

Spica, sparkle, March 15, on Maple Hill, at last. Ear of Wheat in the Virgin's left hand. Now Chaucer's Raven, the Roman Crow, its wings spread toward Barre, carrying Gienah and Algorab. Bootes hunting Ursa. And not only Arcturus, Keeper of the Heaven, Great Horn, but Muphrid, the Officer who accompanies the Emperor. Only in Asia. In the West: he is the solitary one.

Nekkar sits beyond this pair, head of the Hunter, a Female Wolf. The crow forbidden to drink from the cup. The prank she played, leaving her in the sky. From Hittite times. The Bear chased toward the Pole by Hunting Dogs. Gone.

And fall asleep dreaming of Nekkar, of going there, a golden sun, like our own.

*   *   *

Egyptian Face in the Metropolitan Museum of Art

Here I am again, Ka, remembering nothing, as you once promised. Such joy. Such certain presence.

They were touched by you, and you endowed them with light, whose innate fuel we are still burning, our northern wooden idols, our computer maps of your mother's surface in clay. Barely. A seal marking payment in grain.

Those marvellous dead eyes eternity has given us, whose boat we boarded blind, because memory would not have been enough.

You are going, driftweed, to a place that has more than you have ever known.

You are going, spinning top, to a place diminished by what, you will never know. The retreating rays of sunset over the leather arms of the bat. So do I withdraw my holyness now that Egypt is grade silicon sand.

He left instructions that his face be painted on the outside of his coffin so he could see the world. Through my eyes what time has done to the polis and the paint he was painted with, bought with old coins,

from The Planet With Blue Skies / 85

coins still bearing a trace of Atlantean precis.

His dark pupils and curly hair entrusted to Horus, not Marpa, though Marpa yet lives in the blue skies of this planet. But it is Horus whose message brings me here today. Back on the inside, dead wood, again; dead stone. Looking out: whose scarab catches in diorite, whose red buildings begin to crumble in the April breezes. World War I quarries. Stone-setters. So that the meteorite brought from Alaska to the New York City Planetarium is carted up 8th Avenue, Central Park West, from the docks by teams of horses and wagons.

Whose refugees live in these remote art gallery streets. In a suspicion more than the proof by which his image remains. They have seen too much to realize that the jewel has been lost, the gold chain the queen wore, hammered by sizzling water, by Nile and Indus, until a spiritual quality rings from the metal. He has been seen by too many eyes/I have.

As possible as I have made him.

*   *   *

She is there, flawed as the born one. She has that accuracy and raw emergence that leads to a full sky as surely as that first star on the Belt blossoms by night into the full Orion, armed, and if he is Set, Lepus the Hare is his boat. All that plus the constellations we don't even see. I await all that as you have awaited it, with surety and joy.

What you say is true: when I look I see you smiling back at me. So I look.

*   *   *

A flock of geese suddenly overhead. Bright calls that seem to come from some other part of the sky. The sky is large in all directions. They are a single V, having joined at an earlier point because a procession was forming, and now they are in the middle of it, the embodiment of all that must happen, what is in it, before it ends.

The limbs of the V break apart and become small V's themselves, sharing always one side with the larger wedge. The pattern breaks apart and reforms so liquidly there is no moment when the motion is stopped. They are a Y, then a W. There is something intelligent about it, of which you would say, not the intelligence of instinct, or gene-borne telepathy of the group, you would say the scribe finds it in Egypt, at the moment he goes to language, to an unenclosed syllabary, in search of language, because those alphabets we do not know are the only information left to gird the limits of A and Z, of Alpha and Zeta, Aleph and Zayin, where a wall is built in the Andes, a lunar mansion in Cambodia.

So I stop and look straight up, and do not move until they are out of sight. It is more than an omen or a vision. It is things as they are at this moment; and an aerial photograph of being here now would have nothing of the precision that brings these geese over, that these geese maintain. They do not have to carry household gods. They carry a mystery. They do not have to follow the leader. The formation is instantaneous, and breaks apart, to reform, in a swell of conditions as subtle and remote as the nervous strands and sinews beneath dreams. It is not enough to say they are winds and temperature and small biological compasses. They are like floating islands, stars, and they are seen not in light or x-ray or infra-red or the reconstructions of radio noise. When the bird lies smashed on the rock, it is the palace of Kubla Kahn. When all that is left is feathers and bones, it is the vagabond epistle who visits each town a day before Paracelsus. When the sea is driven back into the vase, they will be as large as the eagles whose bodies enclose and derive the stars. For when the flight is over, they will let it fall, entirely and without decree.

*   *   *

Summer sky now. The winter stars are lost. Orion and Taurus are gone, but it is the darkness of the sky where they were, and their memory — that is a more powerful image than their loss. Cassiopeia and Cepheus have passed behind the village, the Dipper is bent over our house. Leo, whose head cleared the moments in winter, is now stretched over the top of the sky. Virgo follows, long and hooked, bearing Spica in its center, dividing the sky with upraised arms. Libra follows, Zuben'ubi. The head of the Scorpion comes from the Brook; Antares has risen by mid-evening. Above him, Serpens, a more powerful image than one would have thought him, his straight signal beacon of stars, like hieroglyphs of some intelligence beyond us. Hercules enclosing a realm, and Lyra, with green Vega, half a wing and body of Cygnus.

Serpens is still most striking. I saw him first returning drunk from a party in the middle of the night and felt his alien presence in the sky. I thought him a ruler; Serpens now does not fulfill the condition of that name, except its pincertop. Ophiuchus, big and shapeless as the heavens themselves are, fills the full sky over Maple Hill, warring even to push the Scorpion from the ecliptic, which itself is not straight but seems to bend and twist away across the sky. A satellite passes through Virgo, bright and swift in the body, then gone into its minor chord of darkness.

It is a depleted sky. The fires of winter are gone. The signs fall where they have shifted, and continue to shift, in unconsciousness, between moments of consciousness, a pattern that unfolds all day and is seen in patchwork nights. The more familiar the sky becomes, the more I will know what the ancients saw in times of change. Eventually winter will come again from Maple Hill, if I wait. And even the fact I know I will not be the same person means it will never come again, that eternal sameness reflecting our passage through it on a particular world in time. That's not what it's there for, but that's forever what it will be in our history. There is no break in the continuity, Greeks and Asians in Palestine, Joshua wandering in trans-Jordan. Bootes. Aquila. The Mayans visiting Florida, selling honey and gold.

*   *   *

Spider dropping, so slowly. Green treelight. Butterfly moth.

Big wet frog.

The clouds hang down so close to this mountain pool, I float on my back kicking, water splashing my eyes, a liquid sun, sparkle. Crack my hollowness. Be full. Down, black and darker and colder and blacker, down into the source of the pool, until it is unbearable.

Jet crashing through clouds.

In a hundred years this will be easy.

Men and women.

Miranda black with mud sitting in the pool of tadpoles Robin has made for her among his earthworks. He runs back and forth with buckets of water, filling the locks. She pours the water on her head.

Salamander frozen at the edge, its body faintly receptive.

Memory of chamomile tea in earth cup this morning.

I wish we could be as soft and gentle as this forever. The single ant, with the grit of his being, carrying the dead bug, red and blood-like, however small, a backdrop, for the largeness of our lives.

I lie in the sand with fantasies of space itself torn like tissue paper. Placing the Earth tangent to the other side. A gigantic map itself reduced to a speck by the brilliance of sun and clouds on this one world, at the other end.

*   *   *

Lemon rays of morning shatter against the glass, small flies rising in dusty light. Hard beetle on its back in the bathroom.

Birds drinking from the puddles, opening their necks to the largeness of the sky.

Three women working in the garden, opening the garden. In soft clothes, bent, passing each other at different speeds. Gentleness of their bare feet in the earth.

Sounds of birds scattered in the landscape. Single petals fall from the apple tree, swirl in the grass with the sawdust.

Far away storms exchange their charges, thunderstorms, galactic storms. Electricity. Here the currents mix.

The din of the city is reduced to a patch, a bare abrasion in the glen. But one whose focus holds like bedrock as the leaves and spaces between the leaves scatter their light.

Intimation of unknown sensors. Rough proximity of stars. The beetle released out the window. The mysteries in their chalice, gestating, old.

The ants arising from an unknown source.

*   *   *

Summer Travels
Going West in July

Denver:
The buffalo in the zoo find their rough primitive bodies set at regular distances. They take journeys to visit each other. They nurse their children in the shadows of their bodies. They are inseparable from shaggy robes.

Wise bearded faces of the elders: they are Indians. They live in a reservation village, untempted by the streets and bars of the city.

Wyoming:
The dusty rock-essences, wind-hollowed, standing as islands in a waterless current of air.

Grey sand streaked with orange and red. Malachite green written into the dust. Everything is worn by wind and light. Machines, like tired bums, dig for oil. Rawlins, as wealthy as it gets, you monopoly town. Whose glittering face: the real slums.

Flashes of purple flowers for brief stretches in the hills, so intense and brief they are memory. Wyoming bright in the lucid air.

The sheep follow trails along the sides of the dusty hills. All that keeps this from being Jerusalem is history.

Salt Lake City:
Water from the mountains running in tunnels past houses into the city. Children's toys in the grass.

The temple streets are enclosed in an ancient Mediaeval sense. The desert, ceaseless surveillance. Ogden one way, Pocatello the other, Laramie back to the East. Head of a single cow sheared off. Lying by the roadside.

So purple it is almost red again, the rose fed by an unusual Utah rain.

Always blue blue sky. Hills up against rocks, broken. Cavities. Sucked off. Every space hollow and negative, until not even that is left. A stub for a monument.

At night the external temple lights, Salt Lake City in the bowl. Aquilla over the fence, and straight above, Lyra, retracing its routes, twists around so that Cassiopeia is over the single mountain, Cepheus dimmer, maintaining the relationship.

The Scorpion a bent arrow, an aged lame worm.

Plane trees, a willow, and the water running in the true endless softness of time, always arriving, July 4th, Virginia 1250 East, Third Avenue North. A single tower stands before the mountain, horizon of another, further west, inland sea.

The Lake:
Swarming insects in the sand. Stingless, we place our feet down in them. They scatter like shadows of soot. Faint green the mountain, just a hint of life left. Not smoke but chemical, expanding slowly as it drifts against the mountains. The gulls as white as the woman's hair. The people, young, elderly, fat, babies, strung out in these shallow revival waters like a photograph of Judgment.

Snackwagon, red and blue. Decayed hose for bathers. The gulls sit on the bare telephone wires, their feathers abalone.

The cars come, in a brief geological era, where rains have filled a bowl. Currentless. Duned. There is something larger and flatter here. All this hammered metal, drawn out of the ground and shaped into balloon-thin cars around simple pipe engines, running off snorts of incomplete fire, is absolutely lucid here. The cars are subterranean; they have been taken from the earth. You can see it, the decay, the end of it, Winnebago Campers, VW buses, Plymouths, Chevrolets, Pontiacs, De Sotos, American explorers around the snackwagon, sharing scraps with the gulls, and the Hacienda Chemical Company, the Spartans pulling trailers.

It is chemical and rusty and industrial in a way the east will never be, and I now prefer it to the beach on the Atlantic because it is unameliorated, unconcealed.

Drifting on my back in the salt, rills pulling back underneath me, a Moon so soft and gentle, its buoyancy is original. Shrimp active in their medium.

Never getting deeper, just walking out and out. How soft, how white, how like feathers, how fine, how salt, it burns my eyes, a softness like gypsum. An acid which is not life but which flows through life. This extreme lake of radiation passing through the bareness of the mountains, rubbed down to copper, decanted through the bodies of the shrimp. Only differential, peristalsis, halts it.

I close my eyes and float, inner eye gulls, the wind light on their feathers, their arms, my fingers, reaching out for an object of meditation.

Desert West:
The single radar station.
White coating on the hardpan. Visible bursts of plants sucking invisible moisture.

Americans leave their names in rock by the roadside. They build cairns and Peace signs and write Jesus in single boulders. The silence is final.

These are testaments to the crudity of intelligence, how like a wedge on the infinite it is. Plus the unevolved creeping. Because silence is always in touch with intelligence, silence precedes it. Scrub by scrub, the sage tender, closer to the stars that milk them than us.

They crack the surface in the one eternal moment of seed, not feeling a thought, but their own coming, which must happen, which must be there, as tiretracks are not. The clump of vegetation on the Great Salt Desert is as large as the jungle ever was. Even what it does not see, it is.

The white at the bottom of the pelican sun, cirrus clouds in a perspectiveless blue refraction, mirror which hides the body. The cumulus sit, guardians of the last water jugs. Succulence they stream with, if we could see it, yellow red blue orange, casting out iris, rainbows, wings.

Our memories would lie flat on these planes forever.

Nevada:

Mexican restaurant, plate of beans, smooth in tacos and enchil-ladas, Olympia Beer. The supermarket open July 4th, I buy diapers and peaches, and we sit in the playground among the dozens of slides, circles, spirals, clowns' faces, rocket ships, our kids run loose through the trees. Voice in the distance announcing the local July 4th game, pitch by pitch.

The sign reads: settlers, railroad, Jaycees. It took something to put such a civilized playground on the desert, that goes as deep as the covers of a hundred comics and science fiction books.

Nevada is great rocks stretched high above the sky, broken in fields, is the casino towns played off that one electric string. Silver dollars everywhere, as if the mint were at hand. Fireworks at twilight out of Battle Mountain, visible against the flatness, we drive for thirty miles watching them change position only gradually until the road is ordered into town by a local judge.

Night. Galaxy so thick, its far robes sweep about the mountains. Scrub and sweet bushes in the air. Lindy driving near dream, we knock off a jack rabbit that bounded from the darkness into our path, leave it in the dark gate of Orion, brief bump up and over its bones, o mes-senger who did not reach us, messenger from the outwash onto the road. Seeing our light. How swiftly we end the connection, how little we are worthy of it. The surety with which you came, Nevada, and are gone.

*   *   *

Returning East in August:

Northern California:

The coastal fog behind us, blue air now blue sky, a single hot white star. The rock rich red around Chico.

Shasta is the center of this system. Shasta carries snow for this entire level of ascension.

Golden light through the mountains, descending through inner acupuncture points. Mountaintops in deep communion of twilight. Rich sparkling water, potentized against the rocks, receiving stars be-fore the stars are visible.

Reservoir leading into lumbertown. Telephone lines following railroad tracks following the river. All these black lines, flak against the blue. Giant express trucks carrying livestock, resonating. Deer leaps in the red field, where, in the distance past, the farmer pulls the cutter. So much timber the water is clogged with it, filled in every length and width and diagonal of the fluctuating present, jammed back up the town, the smell of burnt wood delicious even in its raging pollution. More delicious than potato chips, popcorn, hungrier than beef, as deep and sunny into night as dandelion root tea, where the smoke rises into charged purple sky.

Oregon:

Sage, evaporating. Cooling off after the sweaty day. The stars open cells, sweet through the grills of the car.

North out of Klamath Falls through Bend, up the mountains and down into the tiny town of Maupin, sleepy beyond words, stumbling into a hollow fisherman's cabin, giant metal bed, stringy bedcovers, medicinal smell, rust and paint peeling, and a linoleum floor, barely heated by those few red coils that stare at us all night. This is the darkness and singleness at the center of life, left the the shallow migration westward.

Morning. White cumulus beginning, puffs above the mountaintops, dreams. The trees rushing down to drink from the Deschutes River, bushy in their tops with water. Water underneath, rushing. Roots.

Washington:

The Columbia, carrying this system to the sea. Butteland on the Washington side, flat and open. The Oregon slope littered with basalt. The Columbia where Indians fished, their lives in this mirror the road scrapes silver off. Black and white bird wings, missing heads, missing bodies, stuck to the roadside, blowing limply because there is still resistance.

Insects cluster like a single mind on the vegetation — the Dalles, John Day Dam. Hitting the windshield silently, but cover it entirely.

And the rocks bared, white powder left on them, from the big axes. Oil in pools. Thin points of land go out, small tides, changes of blue, lines stretched through the fluid. Are they lines of temperature or depth? A single dragonfly, our energy. Because things live. Modoc Point. Beyond the cattle farms, the tractors. Old willow next to Shasta

Real Estate. Modoc Restaurant and Grocery, closed, windows broken. Goldenrod in the field, up the base of the mountain. Tough succulents. The rocks underneath, torn up. There is still transmission here: a conch shell from the Pacific Coast, the roads going South to Reno and Winnemucca. The water comes powerfully from my spine into my eyes. It is more than a memory. It is a state of existence.

Idaho:

Crossing the Snake River into Idaho. Famous unknown land. Flushes of green, small gardens and sunflowers twisted around metal, potatoes and corn. The dried up river fossils on the hillsides. Ochre ground. Gentle blue sky.

Yellow straw rules; the green is a network of oases, each like a round flower in the sand. Dark against dry fields. Droplets. Single tree as full as cumulus by the farmhouse, bursting with day.

The run-offs are hidden between hills whose curves flow around each other, overlapping, base and height. The land is so big everything is toylike, the cows emblems, the houses swallowed into unmeasured distances, an acre nothing against the acreage stretching into low bush. Thunderheads piling at least a day's drive away.

Cutters. Bees. Supplies. An amusement fort sitting like an abandoned skee-ball machine in Far Rockaway, false front painted on, more like a candy wrapper. Irrigation canal rises with the rushes, Mormon Nile.

Farm equipment and cows and old machines lying in one splotch of green on a golden planet. The straw tied in bundles. The Eurasian horses depicted in the sun, genetic colors on their sides, flowing muscles as they run on bumps. The sheds connected in series of complicated solids. Icebox, cow standing beside it, tied to its door, drinking from a slosh-box, ass bumping into old tractor. In the distance, black and white running together beside a fence. Yellow and pink flowers climbing a rock wall.

Enormous auto graveyard under the big sky, coming into Boise.

The Giant announcer faint as we move across the Idaho-Utah border, bumping along the patchwork road. Remembering the ballpark in San Francisco, popcorn, perfume, the movements white and clear.

A haste at the end of summer so complete: prairie dogs lie dead by the cactuses. The Moon in a quarry of black clouds. Proving the three-dimensionality of the Earth. Only if you see it that way. And wind. Blowing back the storm. And stars lying below Cassiopeia, stars

I have never seen.

Utah:

The dream is stronger than afternoon. Ivy climbing the tree trunk. Sky richer than a well. Bees moving in the wind, as softly as measuring. You can see the weather lying in chunks out towards the mountains. It is Stone. Clouds come in, pound rain on top of Salt Lake. Industrial dust blows from its moorings and covers the town.

The few skyscrapers in this bowl, temples Crowley called them. Streets named after temples running to the baseline.

Wyoming:

All systems open, cosmos, big bang, U.N. Nomad Inn. New Grand Cafe. A repeating sequence of clouds in the sky. An unrelenting wind.

David Brennan

A Chinese Poem for Dan and Ann

Cows low in the mist
sounding like the hills themselves
moaning, shifting in sleep

We sit in the untended grass
and pursue the three delights
friends know: talk, drink, laughter

Let the idiots spend forever
counting up what they own
We'll be aimlessly drunk in the meadow
and leave the gate open

Susan Howe

from Articulations of Sound-Forms in Time
(1984)

Home in a human knowing

Stretched out at the thrash
of beginning

Sphere of sound

Body of articulation chattering

an Assassin
shabby halo-helmet

hideout haystack hunter chamois

History of seedling and seduction
kinship of infinite separation

Sight of thought

Crooked erratic perception
shoal ruin abyssal veil veiling

Braggart expert
discourse on dice

Face to visible sense gathers moss

Left home to seek Lost

Pitchfork origin

tribunal of eternal revolution
tribunal of rigorous revaluation

Captive crowned tyrant deposed
Ego as captive thought

Conscience in ears too late

Father the law
Stamped hero-partner

pledge of creditor to debtor

Destiny of calamatous silence
mouth condemning me to absence

—Uneasy antic alibi

dimmed dimmest world
final fertile mantle of family

Leap from scratch to ward off

Girl with forest shoulder
Girl stuttering out mask or trick

aria out of hearing

Sound through cult annunciation
sound through initiation Occult

Enunciate barbarous jargon
fluent language of fanaticism

Green tree of severance
Green tree girdled against splitting

Transmutation of murdered Totem

Foresters move before error
forgotten forgiven escaping conclusion

Oak and old hovel grow gossamer

Hemmed trammels of illusion
rooted to shatter random

Firstborn of Front-sea
milestone by name farewell

Milestones bewitched millstones
Sleep passage from Europe

Otherworld light into fable

Negative face of blank force

Winds naked as March
bend and blend to each other

Fledgling humming on pathless

Old Double and old beginning Vain
Covergesture

Summary of fleeting summary
Pseudonym cast across empty

Peak proud heart

Majestic caparisioned cloud cumuli
East sweeps hewn flank

Scion on a ledge of Constitution
Wedged sequences of system

Causeway of faint famed city
Human ferocity

Dim mirror Naught formula

archaic hallucinatory laughter

Kneel to intellect in the work
Chaos cast cold intellect back

acoustic tatters kneeling in speech
acoustic tatters keening structures

acoustic name nation
ivy

Lighthousleas may to manymy

Mikhail Horowitz

Stonehenge

(11/22/72)

Ride w/a stone man in a stone lorry to Amesbury & walk 4
   miles
The joints of the old earth creak; rusty hinge in the green sun
Sky as blue as an echo
& Stonehenge IS the echo   is the EYE of the echo
Midpoint of a lost polarity
The only echo under the sun, dead center
Stealing into the house of holes w/no key, for this is the keyhole
Chipped stairway to stars of stone
& Stonehenge IS the cornerstone   the fluctuant debris of a
   structure no longer standing
A library skyscraper whose letters are lost   whose index cards
   are clouds
Sun's hitching post
A parking lot for Lot's wife
But Stonehenge has not yet turned to salt
A lapidary yawn   A shrug of the old stone shoulders
It PICKS ITSELF UP, IT MOVES
The druid levitates the sun is still & Stonehenge MOVES
The essence of Stonehenge is animal
A stony herd of megalithic cows convening moodily on the moor
They will always convene on the moor
Chewing the ancient cuds of moonlight as Milky Ways curdle to
   cream
To metaphysical hemispheres of half & half
I found a seashell at Stonehenge   Dog whelk from the Dog Star
Imprint of a starfish in the novastone
There are constant arrivals & departures here
Invisible airport   dark things gliding in turbulent air
O stony rush of wings   Spirits & dimmer things alight
   w/parachutes of stone

Stone the bloody crows a scarecrow at Stonehenge
A snowman at Stonehenge
I read the palms of Stonehenge they told me nothing
Nothing to dry on the blue sky clothesline of Stonehenge
Nothing to do & no stone shoe to do it in
For unlike these stony totempoles w/words & numbers in place
    of eyes & ears I have forgotten my face
Face that was a mage's face at Stonehenge
Face that crawled on all fours in the awesome mall of Stonehenge
Like William Blake crawling among the monumental toys in his
    crib
It is not an ephemeral thing
It is no Rube Goldberg contraption
It is the fossil of Adam's ribcage, for "Adam was a Druid"
The ghost of astral clockwork
The sun's first set of teeth
Despite the tourists I worship alone at Stonehenge
Alone w/all the aching slabs of sun
Alone w/all the opening doors of light
Vanishing w/all the volumes of lost knowledge as the sun snakes
    down over Medusa's roofbeams
As Blake walks under a Jacob's ladder
As stalemate settles in violet red magenta on this last incipient
    astrolithic chessboard
I place a lonely metronome at the foot of a standing stone
A footnote to nothing
Night slips a dark key into the sun's hole
Moon is a floating rune
Stonehenge will be the last of the world's power plants to melt
    down
Last of the trees
Last of the libraries
But one bright morning all the books are gone

Mikhail Horowitz

Station 6^2: The Star Cliff

Stratigraphically underlying the astroconglomerate are beds of stars at least ten trillion light years thick. They are composed of consolidated gas and ambergris. Somewhere back in the Mezzrow-zoic, they decided to jazz up a dark and joyless evening by jutting out. So here they are.

And we are their talus, pronounced tay-lus.

Walk 440 light years to the middle of two white fires opposite a gas bank.

You are now at Station 7^2 on your map.

Mikhail Horowitz

Walking Home

Dusk gilding the clouds the road the telephone poles
The ancient songs of William Blake I mull in purple air

Golden boy w/a golden dipstick manning the gas pumps
Exxon is Eternal Delight

Ah, slugs   moist as tongues or genitals unconcealed
Too prolix, they moisten the road's shoulders, unseen
    victims of maneless Pintos

Abandoned penny flashing its teeth of zinc

Fragments of a shattered windshield
Blue trails of a comet that left Detroit 100,000 years
    ago

Queen Anne's face in Queen Anne's lace
Cold sickle of a moon
Tawny autos & amber clouds like genitals unconcealed

Something senior to me is watching me
Guiding me

                                    a lone terrestrial,
home tonight before the Perseids fall

Henri Michaux

Icebergs

(1934)

translated by Jesseca Ferguson

Icebergs, without guardrail, without a belt, where old crestfallen cormorants and the souls of recently dead sailors lean on their elbows in the enchanting nights of Hyperborea.

Icebergs, Icebergs, cathedrals of the eternal winter without religion, covered with the glacial skullcap of planet Earth.

How high, how pure are your borders begot by the cold.

Icebergs, Icebergs, shoulders of the North Atlantic, august Buddhas frozen on uncontemplated seas, scintillant Headlights of Death without egress, the bewildered cry of silence lasts for centuries.

Icebergs, Icebergs, Recluses without need, closed countries, distant and free of vermin. Parents of islands, parents of springs, as I see you, how familiar you are to me . . .

Henri Michaux

I Write You from a Far Away Country

(1938)

translated by Jesseca Ferguson

I)   We have here, she said, only one sun per month, and for a short time. One rubs one's eyes for days in advance. But in vain. Inexorable time. The sun arrives at his own hour.

Then one has many things to do while it's light, so many that one scarcely has time to look at oneself.

The annoying thing is that it's night when we must work, and we must: dwarves are born continually.

II)   When we march in the country, she further confided in him, we sometimes encounter considerable masses in our path. These are mountains and we must sooner or later start to bend our knees. No use resisting, we can't go any further, even by doing ourselves harm.

It's not to wound that I say this. I could say other things if I really wanted to wound.

III)   Dawn is grey here, she said further to him. It wasn't always like this. We don't know who to blame.

In the night the cattle make great crying sounds, long and fluted at the end. You feel compassion, but what can you do?

The odor of eucalyptus surrounds us: blessings, serenity, but it can't save us at all, or do you really think it grows in order to save us?

IV)   I add another word, really a question. Does water also run in your country? (I don't remember if you told me) and it also gives you shivers if it's really water.

Do I love it? I don't know. One feels so alone in water when it's cold. It's totally different when it's hot. So how to judge? How do you judge, you others, tell me, when you speak of water without disguise, with an open heart?

V)   I write you from the end of the world. You should know about this. Often trees tremble. We pick up the leaves. They have a crazy number of veins. But to what end? There's nothing more between them and the tree, and we go off downcast.

Can life on earth continue without wind? Or must everything tremble, always, always?

There are also subterranean movements, and at home like angers which come up in front of you, like severe beings who want to pluck out confessions.

We don't see anything, so it doesn't matter that there's so little to see. Nothing, and yet we tremble. Why?

VI)   We women live here with tight throats. Do you know that even though I'm very young, other times I was still younger, and my companions too. What does that mean? There's surely something awful in that.

And those other times when, as I already told you, we were even younger, we were afraid. One might have profited from our confusion. One might have said to us: "Look, we're burying you. The moment has come." We were thinking: "It's true, we could also easily be buried tonight, if it is vowed that that is the moment."

And we didn't dare run too much: out of breath, at the end of a race, arriving in front of a ditch all ready, and not the time to say a word, not the breath.

Tell me, what then is the secret in connection with all this?

VII)   There are constantly, she told him further, lions in the village who walk about without any constraint. As long as we pay no attention to them, they pay no attention to us.

But if they see a young girl run in front of them, they don't wish to excuse her anxiety. No! Immediately they devour her.

That's why they walk constantly in the village where they have nothing to do, because it's quite evident they could yawn just as well elsewhere.

VIII)   For a long time, a long time, she confided to him, we have been in a debate with the sea. On very rare occasions when she is blue, calm, you'd think her content. But that doesn't last. Her odor, moreover, says it, an odor of rottenness (if it isn't her grief).

Here I must explain the business of the waves. It's madly complicated, and the sea . . . I beg you, have confidence in me. Would

I want to fool you? She is not only a word. She is not only a fear. She exists, I swear to you: one sees her constantly.

Who? Why, we, we see her. She comes from very far away to tease and frighten us.

When you come you will see her yourself, you'll be totally astonished. "Hold on!" you'll say, because she's stupefying.

We'll look at her together. I'm sure that I will not be afraid anymore. Tell me, will this ever happen?

IX)   I cannot leave you in doubt, she continues, with a lack of confidence. I'd like to speak to you of the sea. But there's a problem. The streams advance, but she does not. Listen, don't get mad, I swear it to you, I wouldn't dream of deceiving you. She's like that. As strongly as she agitates, she stops before a tiny bit of sand. It's a great embarrassment. She would surely like to advance, but those are the facts.

Perhaps later, one day, she will go on.

X)   We are more than ever surrounded by ants, says her letter. Restless, full-tilt, they push the dust. They aren't interested in us.

Not one raises its head.

This is the most closed society that there is, although they constantly spread themselves about outside. No matter, their projects, their preoccupations . . . they are amongst themselves . . . everywhere.

And up to the present not one has raised its head to us. It would rather be crushed.

XI)   She wrote him further:

"You wouldn't imagine all that there is in the sky, you'd have to see it to believe it. So look, the . . . but I'm not going to tell you their name right away.

Despite their air of being very heavy and occupying almost all of the sky, they don't weigh, big as they are, as much as a newborn baby.

We call them clouds.

It's true that water comes out of them, but not by compression, or grinding them. That would be useless, since they have so little.

But, because of their occupying lengths and lengths, widths and widths, depths also and depths and of inflating themselves, finally they let fall some little drops of water, yes, water. And one is good and wet. One runs off furious at having been trapped; for no one knows the moment when the drops will be released; sometimes they go for days without releasing them. And one would stay at home waiting in vain.

XII)   Education about shivers is not well done in this country. We are ignorant of the true rules and when the event appears, we are caught unaware.

It's Time, of course. (Is it the same in your country?) One must arrive earlier than He does; you see what I'm saying, just a little bit in advance. You know the story of the flea in the drawer? Yes, of course. And how true it is, isn't it? I don't know what else to say. When are we finally going to see each other?

Jean Genet

The Strange Word Urb . . .

translated by Bettina Knapp

Whether the strange word *urbanism* originates with Pope Urban or the word *city*, it will probably no longer apply to the dead. The living will get rid of their cadavers, surreptitiously or not, just as one does away with a shameful thought. By dispatching them to the crematorium, the urbanized world will do away with tremendous theatrical aids, and perhaps even with the theatre itself. To replace the graveyard in the (perhaps eccentric) center of the city, columbariums will be erected at a distance from the city, with or without chimneys, with or without smoke, and the dead, calcinated like small calcinated loaves, will serve as fertilizer for the kolkhozes or the kibbutzim. Yet, if cremation should take a turn for the dramatic—should one man be burned with solemnity, roasted alive, or should a city or a state wish to rid itself *en masse* of another community—the crematorium such as Dachau evokes a certain possible future, an architectural timelessness which escapes future and past: its chimneys constantly tended by cleaning crews singing lieder around this obliquely erected sex of pink bricks, or simply whistling Mozartian tunes, forever feeding the gaping jaws of an oven where up to ten or twelve cadavers can be placed, then shoved in—a certain kind of theatre can be perpetuated. But if the crematoriums are hidden away or reduced to the dimensions of a city grocery store, the theatre will die. We will ask future urbanists to plan on having one graveyard in each city where the dead can still be buried, or to build a frightening columbarium, in a simple but commanding style, so that a theatre can be erected next to it, in its shadow or among the tombs. Do you see what I'm driving at? The theatre will be placed as close as possible to the truly guardian shadow of this place where the dead lie buried, or close to the solitary monument which digests them.

I am giving this advice with little ceremony. I'm dreaming, really, with the active nonchalance of a child who knows the importance of the theatre.

One goal of the theatre is to help us escape so-called "historical" time, which is really theological time. From the very start of the theatrical event, the time-flow belongs to no calibrated calendar. It escapes the Christian era as it does the revolutionary era. Even if "historical" time (I mean time marked from a mythical and controversial event, called Advent) does not entirely vanish from the spectators' consciousness, another time, with neither a beginning nor an end, unfolds, in which the spectator lives fully: it destroys the historical conventions necessitated by social life and in so doing also destroys social conventions — not in order to create just any kind of disorder, but rather to pave the way for liberation. The dramatic event now suspended — on its own time, outside of recorded time — has led to a vertiginous liberation.

The Christian Occident has done its best, and so very slyly, to ensnare the peoples of the world into believing in an era beginning with a hypothetical Incarnation. It's really nothing more than the "calendar angle" that the Occident tries to impose on the entire world.

Trapped within a given time, recorded from the onset of an event which interests only the Occident, the world runs the great risk, if it accepts this time, of stressing certain celebrations and thereby holding the entire world captive.

It would seem urgent, then, to multiply these "advents," creating new calendars from them, calendars unrelated to that already imperialistically imposed. I think that any event, personal or public, can give birth to many calendars and thus scuttle the Christian era and everything that is connected with a time recorded from the Very Questionable Nativity.

The theatre . . .
THE THEATRE?
T H E   T H E A T R E.

Where do we go from here? Toward what form? The whole theatrical place: the stage and the auditorium?

The place. I told an Italian who wanted to build a theatre with mobile parts and an architecture which would change with the play, even before he finished his sentence, that theatrical architecture still remains to be discovered; but it must be stable, immobilized, and thus accountable — it will be judged on its form. It is too easy to depend on the mobile. Work towards the transitory, if you must, but only after the irrevocable act on which we are judged has been accomplished, the stable act which judges itself.

Since I am devoid of spiritual powers myself (if they exist), I do not require scenic space to be chosen after meditation, by a man or a community capable of it; the architect will have to discover the meaning of the theatre in the world and, understanding it, go about his work with almost priestly and smiling gravity. If need be, let him be protected during the course of his undertaking by a group of men who know nothing about architecture, but who are capable of real audacity—that is, inner laughter—in the meditative effort.

If we accept—provisionally—the common notions of time and history, recognizing that the act of painting altered after the invention of photography, it appears that the theatre will not remain what it was before movies and television. As long as we have known theatre, it seems that each play, aside from its essential function, was stuffed with political, religious, moral, and other preoccupations, transforming the dramatic action into a didactic tool.

Perhaps—and I shall always say perhaps because I am a man and all alone—perhaps television and movies will play a more important role in education; then the theatre will find itself emptied, perhaps purified, of everything that encumbered it; then perhaps it will dazzle with its own quality or qualities—which perhaps still remains or remain to be discovered.

With some exceptions—fragments of pictures—few painters before the discovery of photography have left evidence of a vision and an art freed from the concern for a slavishly observed likeness. Not daring to tamper with the face (except for Franz Hals: *The Regents*), those painters who sought to serve both the painted object and the painting (Velasquez, Rembrandt, Goya) used a flower or a dress as a pretext. Possibly painters were abashed by the results of photography. Afterwards, they went back to work: they rediscovered painting.

Likewise, or similarly, dramatists are abashed by the potential of television and films. If they grant that the theatre cannot match the immense power of T.V. and the movies (is it debatable?), dramatists will discover those qualities intrinsic to the theatre, which perhaps spring only from myth.

Politics, history, demonstrations of classical psychology, even an evening's entertainment will have to give way to something else . . . I don't know quite how to describe it . . . perhaps something more brilliant. Then all this dung, this liquid manure will be evacuated. We will have learned that dung and liquid manure are not dirty words. These words, and the situations they evoke, are very numerous in my theatre because they are "forgotten" in most plays; taboo words and situations have impressed themselves upon my plays, sought refuge with me, where they have received the right of asylum. If my theatre stinks, it's because the other is perfumed.

The drama—that is, the theatrical act at the moment of enactment—this theatrical act cannot consist of just anything but it can take anything as its pretext. It seems to me indeed that any event, visible or invisible, if isolated (that is, a fragment of the continuum), can, if properly handled, serve as the pretext or even the point of departure and arrival for the theatrical act. If an event, in one way or another, sets a fire burning within us, the flames rise only after it is stirred up.

Politics, entertainment, morality, etc. need not preoccupy us. If they should slip into the theatrical act despite us, hunt them out until all traces are gone; it's all slag, good for the movies, T.V., cartoons, dime novels—ah, there is a graveyard for these old automobile carcasses.

What about the drama itself? Once the author knows his radiant roots, he must capture this lightning and, from the moment of illumination which reveals the void, construct a verbal (i.e., grammatical and ceremonial) architecture which artfully indicates that an aspect has been ripped from the void which reveals the void.

Let us note in passing that the attitude of Christian prayer (lowered eyes and head) does not encourage meditation. It is a physical attitude which reflects a closed and submissive intellectual attitude; it discourages the spiritual quest. If you choose such a position, God can come upon you, afix Himself right on the nape of your neck, leave His mark which might remain for a long time. In order to meditate, you have to have an open attitude—not one of defiance, nor one of surrender to God. You have to be very careful. A bit too much submission and God sends you His grace: you're screwed.

In today's cities (alas, only on the periphery), the only place a theatre could be built is in a graveyard. This choice will benefit both the graveyard and the theatre. The theatre architect will not put up with the silly structures where families inter their dead.

Raze the chapels. Save a few ruins, maybe: a part of a column, a pediment, the wing of an angel, a broken urn, just to indicate that a vengeful indignation willed this first drama. Let vegetation, and perhaps a sturdy grass, born from the ensemble of rotting bodies, level the field of the dead. If a site is reserved for the theatre, audiences coming and going will have to walk the paths which skirt the tombs. Imagine the spectators leaving after Mozart's *Don Giovanni*: walking away past the dead lying in the earth before re-entering the world of the profane. Neither conversations nor the silences would be the same as the letting out of a Parisian theatre.

Death would be closer and at the same time lighter — the theatre, graver.

There are other reasons. They are more subtle. It is up to you to discover them within yourselves, without defining or naming them.

The monumental theatre — the style is yet to be found — must be as important as the Department of Justice, monuments erected to the dead, cathedrals, the Chamber of Deputies, the Military School, the seat of government, those clandestine areas where the black market and drug traffic flourish, the Observatory. And its function must include all these things at the same time, but in a particular way: in a cemetery or very near to the crematorium with its stiff, oblique, and phallic chimney.

I'm not talking about a dead graveyard, but a living one — that is, not one in which only a few steles remain. I'm talking about a graveyard where graves are being dug all the time, where the dead are being buried; I'm talking about a crematorium where cadavers are being roasted night and day.

Not having spent much time thinking about the theatre, it seems to me that the important thing is not to multiply the number of performances for the benefit (?) of a great number of spectators, but with each public attempt — called a rehearsal — to work toward a single performance whose intensity and brilliance would be so great as to set something ablaze within each spectator, sufficient to illuminate those who had not participated in the performance itself, and to violently agitate them.

As for the audience, only those capable of taking a midnight stroll through a graveyard, ready to meet a mystery, would come to the theatre.

If such an arrangement were made, resulting from urbanism as well as culture, authors would be less frivolous; they would think twice before having their plays performed. They would perhaps be marked for mad, or at least for frivolity verging on madness.

With a sort of easy grace, cemeteries, after a certain time, let themselves be dispossessed. When burials no longer occur, cemeteries die, but in an elegant way: lichen, saltpeter, and moss cover the flagstones. A theatre built in a cemetery will die perhaps — be extinguished — in the same way. Perhaps it will disappear? The theatre might disappear one day. You have to accept this. If someday man's activities become revolutionary, day after day, the theatre will have no place in life. Or if utter dullness leads men to constant dreaming, the theatre will die.

It's stupid to search for the theatre's origins in History, and the origins of History in time.

What would you lose if you lost the theatre?

What will cemeteries be like? An oven capable of decomposing the dead. If I speak of a theatre amid tombs, it's because the word *death* today is tenebrous; and in a world which seems to move merrily towards analytical clarity, with nothing, not even a Mallarmé, to protect our translucid pupils, I think we must add a shadowy note. Science deciphers everything or seeks to; but we are at the end of our rope! We must seek refuge somewhere other than in our ingeniously lighted bowels . . . no, I'm wrong: not seek refuge, but discover a fresh and torrid shadow which will be our work.

Even if the graves become indistinct, the graveyard and the crematorium will be well kept. By day happy crews — Germany has them — will whistle as they clean but whistle in tune. The inside of the oven and chimney can remain black with soot.

Where did I read that in Rome — but maybe my memory is failing me — there was a funeral-mime? What was his role? He led the cortege; he was in charge of miming the most important facts in the dead man's life when he — the corpse — was alive.

To improvise gestures, attitudes?

The words. Living (I don't know how) the French language dissembles and reveals the war of words — enemy brothers, they tear at each other or fall in love with one another. If tradition (*tradition*) and treason (*trahison*) are born from the same original and divergent impulse, each to live its strange life, how do they always know, linguistically speaking, that they are bound together in their distortion?

Now worse than any other, this language, like others, permits cross-breeding of words, like animals in heat; and what emerges from our mouths is an orgy of words which copulate, innocently or not, giving French discourse the appearance of a healthy forest where all animals capriciously flock together. In such a language, you write, you speak, you say nothing. In the midst of this contorted and variegated vegetation, with its mixed pollens, its haphazard graftings, its suckers and slips, teeming and estranged by a deluge of beings, you can only add to the swarm of equivocal words, like the animals in the Fable.

If someone still hopes to write something coherent in the midst of such a proliferation — a luxuriance — of monsters, he's mistaken: at best he can couple larval and deceitful herds (resembling processions of army worms) who would gladly swap their sperm to be able to fertilize just such a carnivalesque, unimportant brood, coming from Greek, Saxon, Levantine, Bedouin, Latin, Gallic, one lost Chinaman, three Mongolian vagabonds, who all speak but say nothing, who reveal by coupling, a verbal orgy without meaning, not in the night of time, but in an infinitude of tender or brutal mutilations.

And the funeral-mime?

And the theatre in the graveyard?

Before burying the dead man, carry the corpse in his casket to the front of the stage; let his friends, enemies, and the curious sit in the section reserved for the audience; let the funeral-mime who led the procession divide and multiply, let him turn into a theatrical company, and let him re-create the life and death of the dead man, right in front of the corpse and the audience; afterwards, let the casket be carried to the grave in the dead of night; let the audience finally leave — the feast is finished. Until another ceremony, occasioned by another corpse whose life is worthy of a dramatic performance — not a tragic one. Tragedy must be lived, not played.

If we are clever, we can pretend we feel at ease; we can pretend the meanings of words remain the same, static, or that they change in obedience to us: we pretend to deliberately modify their meanings just slightly—in this, we become gods. As for me, when confronted with the enraged, encaged herd in the dictionary, I know that I have said nothing and will never say anything. And the words don't give a damn.

Actions are no more docile. There is a grammar for action as there is for language: let the autodidact beware!

Treason (*trahison*) may fit into tradition (*tradition*), but betrayal allows no respite. It took great strength on my part to betray my friends: the reward was waiting for me at the end.

For the great parade, just before the corpse is buried, the funeral-mime, if he wants to re-create the life and death of the dead man, will have to discover and dare to utter, in front of an audience, those dialectophagous words which will devour the dead man's life and death.

Georg Trakl

The Sun

translation by Thomas Frick

Every day the yellow sun comes over the hill.
The forest is beautiful, the hidden animal,
The man: hunter or shepherd.

The fish rises, red in green pond.
Under the circular sky
The fisherman runs smoothly in blue boat.

The grape ripens slowly, the corn.
When the hushed day bows
Good and Evil are brewed.

When night comes,
The wanderer lightly raises his heavy eyelids;
Sun breaks out from the gloomy ravine.

Georg Trakl

Evening in Lans (second version)

translation by Thomas Frick

Journeys through black summer
Past shocks of yellowing grain. Under the whitewashed arch,
Where the swallow played, we drank fiery wine.

Beautiful: purple laughter, and melancholy.
Evening and the dark fragrance of foliage
Shiver our fevered brows.

Silver water covers the steps of the forest,
Nighttime still-life, struck dumb.
Friend: the leaf-covered paths in the village.

Georg Trakl

Night

translation by Thomas Frick

I sing you, wild chasm,
In night-storm
Mountain range vaulting up,
Gray towers
Brimming with hellish grimaces
Passionate beasts
Rugged ferns, fir trees,
Crystalline flowers.
Endless torment,
That you, gentle one,
Hunted for God
Hearing His sigh in the waterfall,
In the surging pinetrees.

The fire blazes up golden
The nations wrestle.
The glowing whirlwind
Plunges, death-drunk,
Over blackened crags,
The blue wave
Of the glacier,
And the bell in the valley
Booms potently:
Flames, curses
And the dark
Games of voluptuousness,
A stone head
Storms heaven.

José Argüelles

Planet Art Report
For Desperate Earthlings of the Past

Although its behavior may seem random or even perverse much of
the time, the art of our planet is a fluid system, subject to natural laws
governing the behavior of all matter and energy. Aided by tools such
as computers, radar, and satellites, we have extended our ability to
express art and have come to understand that its behavior involves
myriad interactions from the microscopic to the global, extending to
the sun and interplanetary space.

Planet art first emerged during the last Ice Age. With the onset
of the holocene era over 12,000 years ago it became an integral feature
of human culture. First through ritual, then through monumental
temple building and the related crafts, planet art began to articulate
the convective flow of culture at certain key points on the planet:
Egypt, Mesopotamia, India, Greece, China, Mexico and Peru. This
flow spread, creating cultural interactions of varying sorts, and finally
expanded to cover the globe through an electrical network of increasing subtlety and sophistication.

It was during the period of global industrialization (1800-2000
AD) that planet art underwent its greatest transformation. Despite
some valid experimentation, in general all local systems were disrupted
by the intrusion of machine industry and electronic media. In nations
of the capitalist economic persuasion art was translated into commercial
enterprise; artists were encouraged to compete rather than to associate
collectively. In nations where a communist economy prevailed, art
became the tool of state propaganda and was expressed through out-
moded bourgeois forms.

By 1967 a major crisis erupted. In the capitalist centers art reached
a condition of Maximum Commercial Entropy. In the communist
centers a massive artists' strike brought about a condition of Total
Aesthetic Stalemate. These phenomena were symptomatic of the larger
situation, the Great Global Crisis of the last two decades of the 20th
century, during which the collapse of most social systems, aggravated

by increasing warfare and by economic breakdown, all but put an end to Global Industrial Civilization.

It was at this time that a genuinely planetary art came into existence. It all began in the fateful year, 1987. Significantly enough, the initial activity occurred in conjunction with the National Center for Atmospheric Research (NCAR) facility in the foothills of the Rocky Mountains in the heart of the North American Continent. As the nerve center of one of the most sophisticated planetary scientific networks, charged with monitoring global and extra-terrestrial climatic changes, the NCAR facility had become increasingly vital after the intensifying volcanic and seismic activity that resulted in the monumental Pacific Tectonic Plate Shift of 1986.

Two pioneer groups operating in the NCAR area met during the first new moon of February 1987: Explorers of the Richness of the Phenomenal World (ERPW) and the World Union of the Guardians of Aesthetic Evolution (WUGAE). Through a contract with NCAR, the two groups were able to use the vast communication system to begin uniting artists in other major planetary centers, thus instituting the Global Arts Monitoring Mission Act (GAMMA). Through this Act, the ERPW and the WUGAE successfully put together and communicated the famous Planetary Art and Energy Bulletin of 1987. As the foundation of all succeeding artistic activity, the basic points of that Bulletin are worth repeating here:

1. Art is a function of energy. Given the unity of humankind as a single planetary organism, art is the expressive connective tissue binding together the individual organisms through energy transformations focussed in the emotional centers of those organisms. Emotional energy is the expressive or outward moving manifestation of vital or biopsychic energy. Properly catalyzed through form, rhythm, color, light, sound, and movement, emotional energy is directly related to the establishment of a dynamic equilibrium with the other forces of the phenomenal world, from the microscopic to the galactic levels. In other words, there can be no proper management of energy at whatever level and for whatever use without bringing into proper deployment the energy system of art. When art disfunctions all systems ultimately disfunction. According to William Blake, 'Art degraded, Imagination denied, War governs the Nations.'

2. No genuine art without transformation of self. Given the nature of art as a function of energy, we find that art, energy and health are

integrally related. If the maker of art is not convinced of his or her own sanity and basic goodness and is not working on ways to bring his or her total being into line with the universal energy spectrum, then the resultant art effect (artifact) will be incomplete and quite possibly destructive of health. Transformation of self is alignment of personal organismic energy with the total energy spectrum, coupled with the acquisition of whatever skills are necessary to communicate quality and depth of feeling and insight through whatever means.

3. Openness of individual breeds collective aesthetic association. The individual creating art not to satisfy personal ambition but to serenely and openly express the universe as he or she experiences it inevitably develops an inclusive attitude i.e. that art should communicate with and include as wide a range of audience members as possible. Universal feeling being inclusive rather than exclusive, the artist also seeks out the possibility of aesthetic enhancement through collective association with other like-minded individuals. This sets the basis for cooperative artistic efforts.

4. Universality of planet art includes past and future in present moment. Art being the expression of energy, the great monuments of past art are actually present moments in the expressive connective tissue of planet art. The pyramid structures of Giza, Teotihuacan, Borobadur; the Ajanta caves; the Acropolis; Chartres Cathedral; Chinese landscape painting; the Mosques of Isfahan all comprise a network of points of aesthetic transmission. The energy of which they are a repository continues to broadcast. Their transmissions are nutrients adding to the health of the organism. Their form and structure provide keys to the development of the post-industrial planet art system. New forms such as radiosonic architecture (combining visual light structure and sound) integrate past energy and future vision. Future vision is simply that which is born out of a concern for what will benefit the greatest number of people for as many generations to come as is conceivable.

5. The recognition of art as a planetary network vital to the functioning of the human organism considered as an interrelated whole is a factor in establishing the basis for a new planetary social order. The planetary organism has been mutating beyond its present anarchic, pre-holistic limitations and planet art is actually a tool facilitating the present transformation. The primacy of art will be established and new, more healthy and beneficial modes of living will replace the sterile assembly line activities of the Industrial Transition. Making full use

of the education and leisure activities made possible by computer technology, planet art provides non-threatening forms of contemplation and action. Drawing on lessons learned from the excesses of ancient monarchy and industrial democracy, planet art can present aesthetic forms rooted in organic hierarchical patterns of nature. Utilizing electronic communications it can monitor these visions on a global scale. Thus, while we have entered a prolonged stage of political anarchy and barbarism, planet art can present a unified vision. This will be of immense help in the long period of reconstruction that lies ahead.

6. Those forming into Planet Art Associations must do so through a common regard for the deeply spiritual nature of humankind. Without this faith in humanity's basic goodness and capacity for transformation, planet art will falter on the shoals of war and the selfish crimes of the past.

These are the main points of the Planet Art Bulletin of 1987. Cautiously transmitted through a loosely connected consortium of Planet Art Associations, these measures provided a large degree of positive vision and spiritual delight through the Seven Dark Centuries which preceded the formation of the Planetary Assembly of Earth Guardians, when a total flowering of planet art finally took place. Finally reconciled with the Global Council on Energy Transformations, the Planet Art Association may now safely declare that Planet Earth has been realized as a work of art.

PAEG, Central Council
Summer Solstice, 735 AH (After Hiroshima)

José Argüelles

Planet Art Report
From Romantic to Geomantic:
An Art Planet Weather Report

"In Velatropa Far away
though devoid of mind's full sway
in measured form with rhythmic heart
all that's done is done as art."

Report filed: AhKa IV, Commander, Space
Cocoon Surveillance Spore, Velatropan
Vector
To: Central Hierarch Vanguard, Arcturus 108x.

I realize I have been sorely remiss in my reports for a number of centuries now — on Velatropa 24.3, called by the locals "earth," a hundred revolutions around the central star comprise a century. In any case, it is imperative that you receive an update on critical developments occurring on the Art Planet, Velatropa 24.3.

It's been some five centuries now since the intelligence here attained incipient globalization — but under the greediest and most spurious of circumstances. Gold and the need for ideological domination, that's what brought it about. Disgusting!

Within two centuries mechanized industrialization was established, and with that event — goodness, did that speed things up! — the collective art spores all but disintegrated. All knowledge became bent to the end of increasing materialism. When material goods can't be acquired by forthright plunder or diplomacy, then it's war. In fact, I have been appalled at the degree to which war has replaced the arting ends of this planet.

But don't let me get ahead of myself. I should say a few more words about the manner in which Velatropa 24.3 has arted.

It took some four billion stellar revolutions of cooling off and numerous biospheric experimentations before this planet evolved a type of being skillful enough to carry the art enzymes and to deploy them in a manner beneficial to the establishment of a unitary consciousness.

Beginning some 50,000 stellar revolutions ago, through the medium of these beings — they call themselves human or earthlings — the planet began to art in a consistent manner. Having spread a fine membrane of art over the planet, well over one hundred centuries past, these beings initiated experiments in agriculture. This provided the base for what they came to call "civilization." There were six independent sites where this civilizing process erupted on the planet surface. Though "individual" civilizations were generally unaware of all of the others, and hence each developed a false sense of uniqueness, from the Arcturian perspective, there is no question that civilization is a single planetary phenomenon. What distinguishes civilization as a geological phase of Velatropa 24.3, is its artfulness. As humans are the civilizing carriers of the art enzyme, artiers is the rightful name for these beings.

Well, not meaning to be tedious or redundant, suffice it to say that these artiers, more unconsciously than consciously, for several thousand stellar revolutions, through their civilizing efforts, allowed the planet to art in a variety of styles and forms. Though the aggressive behavior known as war inevitably developed as a result of the false sense of territorial uniqueness, still, there was enough down here of what's called a "spiritual force" to keep things in balance.

All of that changed, ironically enough, with the onset of incipient globalization. As I've already mentioned, with the spread of industrialization, it seemed almost certain that war would replace art, and with that seal the Art Planet's doom.

During this dark, downward turn of events, a handful of artiers rose to the occasion of championing art as the Voice of the Earth. These industrial age artiers came to be known as romantics. This strange, half-demented lot of misfits intoxicated by the pathos of their own situation, nevertheless kept alive the flame of art. At least, they were moved by some recollection of human vision cooperating with the urges of the earth . . . and this was much more than could be said of the Dark Lords of Matter who ascended to power at that time . . .

However, by the dawn of the third century of industrialization, following a disastrous war (World War I, they called it), even the romantic began to stray, dear me, into the confused byways of his mind, choked with the weeds of disparate and erroneous concepts. Trapped as they were in urban zones, these romantics, sadly enough, had begun to lose touch with the Voice of the Earth.

Following the indescribable turning point of Hiroshima culminating their "Second World War," (my, such a pathetic misuse of globalization!) most of the originally romantically inspired artiers had lost contact with the Voice of the Earth, not to mention the Starry Dynamo of Night!

As the romantic pose turned into urban guerilla art dogma, the need became ever more clear: if the Art Planet was to attain its true destiny, a new call had to be issued. Instead of romantic, the downtrodden, starving, rebellious artier needed a new image, a new role, a new sense of purpose . . .

It was just at that moment, when the basest minds held the highest positions in planetary affairs and were befuddling people's lives with threats of total war known as "peace through strength," that the newly formed Planet Art Network (PAN) issued its first RTA Weather Report, "The Romant-Geomant Transposition." So let us turn to that decisive geomantic proclamation for a brighter take on a great evolutionary moment for our old favorite, the Art Planet, Velatropa 24.3:

Psychoatmospheric Weather Report #1

Issued by: RTA Contingent, Planet Art Network. Romant-Geomant Transposition.

Attention! Feedback received from the Global Memory Bank straddling the soft underbelly of the Van Allen Radiation Belt indicates the dispersal of a psychic weather front of unprecedented magnitude.

As we now know, the last major psychic weather front precipitated by the transition from a stage of mystic exaltation to a focus on means of industrial production resulted in a peculiar quickening of the art enzyme. This desperately adopted quickening manifested in the artier type: romantic. The new psychic weather front currently blanketing the biosphere augers a decisive transposition from the Post-Atomic Romantic to Synthesizing Geomantic, otherwise known as the Romant-Geomant Transposition.

While the Post-Atomic Romant Front is dissipating in confused pockets of entropic individualism, the new Front is effecting a synthesis of all previous stages manifest by the art enzyme. At the same time, the naturally occuring synthesis is synergizing a re-grouping of artiers into collectives known as Art-Spores.

Since the focus of the Art-Spores is the harmonious and skillfully compassionate uplifting of the total planet, to the end of enabling it to cast its VOTE (Voice of the Earth) among other luminaries in this galaxy, the new Front takes on the designation, Geomantic. Sprouting from the timelessness of the Aboriginal Continuity, geomancy refers to the process of divining, knowing, and acting through signs, lines, and designs manifest by planet earth.

Through the classic agricultural civilizations and the subsequent era of mystic exaltation, geomancy provided the perfect fusion between what were later to be called art and science. It was only during the dreadful Industrial Ascendency that geomancy all but disappeared as a legitimate force in the unfolding of civilization. Only the romantic had any recollection of the force and nature of geomancy. Yet even for the romantic, geomancy was much more a matter of nostalgia than a truth to be acted upon. But all of that is over now.

With the issuance of this Weather Report, we, the RTAs — Resident Terrestrial Agents — sound the alert: this is the moment of the Romant-Geomant Transposition! Since there is no man or woman who does not possess the art enzyme, there is virtually no one incapable of responding to the advent of the Geomant Front. Only the build-up of psychic hardware from previous stages can determine how long it will be before a given individual will respond to the Synthesizing Geomant Front. In the meantime, those whose perceptual passageways are not so sand-bagged by materialistic distortions are now being imprinted with the dire but joyous responsibility to join in the process of amalgamating into Art-Spores.

Take heed, and have no fear! Join the ranks of the RTAs in forming the Planet Art Network! Art Now! War no More! With the heart of a warrior, make the art that heals! No split between art and life, art and science, art and politics! Art is the way of the RTA! Know who you are! The Geomant Front is already upon us! Art Now! War no More!

This Weather Report issued in benign aspiration for the intelligent furtherance of all sentient beings.

Well, beloved CHV, that encapsulates my own Report. Since the broadcasting of the RTA Weather Report, my work is certainly going to go somewhat easier. After all, it is always with the greatest gratification that we observe another planet casting its VOTE!

José Argüelles

Baiame's Crystal Pyramid Keyboard: It's the Earth's Turn

It's the EARTH's TURN
The EARTH is TURNing
The EARTH's TURN is BEyond hemispheric balancing
The EARTH's TURN is a wave motion through mind-space
with definite GEOlogical conclusions and conCussions
It's the EARTH's TURN
The only WAY to handle this TURN
for we've already had our TURN
is to SYNCH IN & to SYNCH DOWN
to let it SINK IN, SYNCH down, and so forth
the MYTH IS NOT INVENTED BUT PRESENTED
the MYTH is a RESONANT STRUCTURE
with TELLURIC and COSMIC stations
the MYTH is a STRUCTURE that allows us to RESONATE at all
    levels at ONCE
through RESONANCE we are in FORMED
the in FORMATION structure and the OPERATIVE structure
ARE THE SAME
and the RECEPTIVE mold is NO DIFFERENT than the
    INFORMATION/OPERATIVE STRUCTURE
do you SEE?
BAIAME places the CRYSTAL PYRAMID in the KEYBOARD
    OF THE SUN
DON EDUARDO CALDERON lets the wind touch the bowl of
    water
ripples of EARTH's turning SWEEP
across the empty MIRROR of the PATIO ORACLE
WE ARE BONDED BY THE INFINITE PRESSURE OF EGOLESSNESS
EAGLE CATCHER synchs the MOMENT into the SHADOW cast
by the SMILE of the untutored PRESENT
INDISTINGUISHABLE from the ROCKS and the LIZARDS the

STAR BROTHERS & SISTERS
HAVE ALL IMPLANTED
Their BEING HERE has erased the distance between PERU,
AUSTRALIA
ARCTURUS AND ANTARES
THIS IS KNOWN to me
the ROCK teaching LICHEN the matrix of PATIENCE
THIS IS KNOWN TO ME the crystal geometer
measuring light waves with liquid compass
THIS IS KNOWN TO ME the arbiter of immortality
the convenor of CROWS
the gatherer of DAWNSTARS increasing the HEART's ORBIT
the EMITTER of RADIOSONIC INSECT hosts
thriving on the MOON's ONLY DAUGHTER
HER BONES rolling softly on the OCEAN's IMPERTURBABLE
FLOOR
and as BAIAME   swallows the quartzite obelisk
THE EARTH TURNS
THE HEROES AWAKEN   THE SUNMAIDENS DANCE
and THE FLOWERS OF EVERY FOREST GLEAM
their ASTRAL PETALS SHOWERING LIGHT TO EVERY STONE
the RAINDROPS flying upward to the CLOUD
where ANGELS practice   the GRAMMAR OF BAIAME'S CRYSTAL
SINGING   CHANTING ALL AS ONE
its the EARTH'S TURN

pan 24
7/26/84   38 AH
boulder

José Argüelles

within the EARTH . . .

Within the EARTH we know
　　　　there is an other EARTH
　　　　　This other EARTH
　　　　　　　　knows us
　　　　　　　　though we know it not
　　　　　to make known this other EARTH
　　　　　　　　this present EARTH now opens out
　　　　　　　　and like a flower that has given all
　　　　　　　　provided every bee its suck
　　　　　　　　dis
　　　　　　　　　　integrates
　　　　its petals over-ripe
　　　　　　　　blown apart
　　　　　　　　swept away
　　　　　　　　are now messages
　　　　　　　　carried by a strange and ancient wind
　　　　　　　　to land as fragments of time regained
　　　　　　　　on who-knows-what other worlds
And in its stead
　　　　　this other EARTH
　　　　　　　　now stands revealed
　　　　　　　　not a flower like the last
　　　　　　　　but as a crystal
　　　　　　　　this other EARTH
　　　　　　　　　　both new
　　　　　　　　　　and yet without beginning
　　　　　　　　　　scintillates
　　　　　　　　　　its pattern
　　　　　　　Geometries of secrets
　　　　　　　　　　sown by millenial star-gazers

spontaneously push through
the crust of illusion
separating past from future
This other EARTH beckons
a home more familiar
than the suburban ravage
of plywood and cement
we now call home
this other EARTH
O bounteous crystal gridwork
veins of light connecting sea and
mountain cloud
waiting so long to become VISIBLE
at last pierces the dark tent of sleep
where a race of AMNESIACS
struggleS to ascend
the luminous sound cloud-ladder
leading to the once-and-always
Palace
of Universal Memory
YES
within this EARTH
there is an other EARTH

crystal liberation
of no-more self
the sound so pure
that rainbows cease to disappear

Phil Sittnick

from Bight

Not a sphere
the figure
of the Earth
has a shape
all its own
from the weight
of the waters
it holds in its spin.
The surface
of the ocean
is farther from
its center
at some points
than at others
not a sphere.
The gravitational attraction
of emerged land
causes a heaping-up
of the sea
along continental
and other coasts.
The earth has
a shape
all its own.

Gull

a
low
glide
over
the
primordial
marsh,
seeking
the
succulent,
the
soft
moist
interior
of
things,
its
world

Vessels
on
the
quivering
sea

in
the
very
core
of
me

cargo
in
the
Body
of
the
World

"Plenitude is our condition"

Cross the dunes
are here and there
dotted:

low scrub pines, aromatic bayberry
beach plum, beach grass, loose strife
wild dusty miller

a cover
for the birds
come and go

as the tides and winds
as
the multitude
of gods who

Slight spasms in the muscles
of our hearts

deer in the dunes
to our left and right

an owl white and wary
on a lone phone pole

flood-tide rolling high
the swaying eel grass

tensions on the surface
of our skins:

offerings from the inclusive world
in which we stare

held, absorbed
in the eye's unerring acts

the facts and completions
of the body and the mind

dead pup harbor seal
half-hidden in the winter sand

Rise and fall
of the Merrimack waves

the white stern-lights
of other boats
speckling the distant dark space

only to say
I am here or I am
here

Mit Mitropoulos

38° 22′ N 22° 23′ E

I am putting down a few notes regarding my activity in the deserted area 38° 22′ North 22° 23′ East, for use in your publication, together with a number of illustrations.

A.   The area is next to my place of origin. The settlement goes back to 2000 BC, is a small port that played an important role in the recent past of the sailship era, now only accommodating yachts in transit. The area can be entered after 30 minutes[1] walk from the human settlement called Galaxidi.

This means easy daily access for myself, whilst everybody else is put off, both because they prefer other locations accessible by boat (38° 22′ N 22° 23′ E can be approached by small boat on very few positions only) or car/motorcycle (38° 22′ N 22° 23′ E isn't crisscrossed by networks of roads or paths, and would be difficult to construct either).

B.   The deserted waterline landscape suggested, almost imposed on me a ritual approach to whatever activity I started on it right from the beginning, summer 80. Since then, each year, before I start on whatever activities I have planned (some upon demand, such as for a particular show) I begin by first wooing the site by a series of other activities.

This attitude towards the site makes it necessary to select those that I may bring along on the site: there is the rare maximum of a group of 4 and myself, all of course relating to me by some form of common activity, but usually it is one other besides me, often enough a model.

C.   By now, the area bears the marks of *Apotypomata* (traces, imprints) resulting from those activities (objects or symbols, as well as names for the various places) and also of the To-Be-Found activities (more objects or symbols left there so as to be found by the odd person crossing the area).

Such To-Be-Found activities pose questions relating to the presence of an audience. Andre Malraux would probably say that such communications are addressed to the angels alone, but what I do is to assume a potential audience itself in awe of the deserted area. Such an audience has already been filtered through the necessary effort to get there, after he/she has made the decision to do so in the first place.

D. Part of what I find there I also use there. Other material I do bring in myself, whether the result of activity elsewhere, or what I receive over the mail or even solicit myself through the mail art network.

Several cultural objects may be produced on site (e.g. drawings or photos) others require follow-up activity elsewhere (e.g. processing images through a videosynthesizer, or casting bronzes).

Last summer and fall 84, I concentrated on Found objects that you could also eat (e.g. any octopus, mussels) and of course herbs (e.g. wild peartree leaves, and especially thyme). Along the area you may also come across the odd beast (goat or fox, dead or alive) and even rarer a human being. Having started to systematically collect and record obsidian pieces has resulted in locating an obsidian prehistoric workshop for making tools. Lots of flakes, less blades, some cores, and plenty of the resulting prehistoric garbage take the human settlement back a few thousand years more.

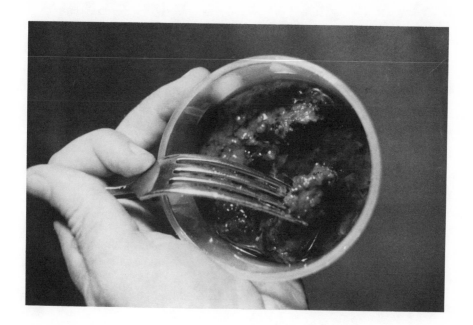

MIT: *Number One* is with this idea of having a found object which you can then eat. Edible found objects. The concept of found being one of the three concepts I've been working with. Found object; the concept of *Apotypomata* which is the concept of doing a *trace*, an imprint; and then the third which is the real/unreal. The real/unreal is the situation of theatricality. The more sophisticated the culture, the more conceptual the culture, the more real/unreal it is. So American culture is obviously more real/unreal than a Greek village. Number one is the cooked octopus. I found the octopus dried, drying in the sun, obviously somebody had caught the octopus, and had left it there to dry up.

TF: That's something that people do?

MIT: Yes. That's one way to do it. Spread it out and leave it in the sun. But this of course was on the edge of the deserted area. So it was not something that you leave there and come back to get. Obviously it was forgotten. There must have been other stuff that this fellow had caught and left.

   Number Two is a wintertime found object to be eaten. It is olives, so this was during the November-January period. This is on the moun-

tain of the deserted area. The salt that shows white on the olives is also found there. What happens is you have some rock cavities which are not very deep, and not very shallow. And they have to be on the side of the area that is hit by the waves, on the northern wind. The waves hit the rocks, they go up and spray, and then wind brings the spray into those cavities. Then, you have to follow up the windy period with a dry sunny period. This will make the water evaporate, and you have flat sections of salt. The temperature under the salt is hotter than the outside. I've been measuring this. A kind of scientific collection of data. Although these data do not have a scientific objective. It's simply observing things in a systematic way.

TF: Did you find the olives on the tree?

MIT: Yes. The olives are on the tree, and the way we do it, we get this cloth which permits air to come in and out, and we cover the olives with the salt. We leave them there for three or four weeks and every other day we give it a good shift, so the olives and the salt will move about. Three or four weeks later they are ready to eat.

TF: Are they green when you pick them?

MIT: No. They are wine-red. Wine-blue. Wine red-blue. It's like the color of the sea. A kind of very dark blue with a bit of red. It's beau-

tiful. They're also very interesting to touch. A lot of the found objects to eat are very interesting to touch.

Like this image *Number Three* which is the mussels. The mussels
come on the interface of the water and the land, the area where the
water shifts back, where you have high tide/low tide. A lot of beasts
habitate in that slice of high tide/low tide. The way people usually
do it is they wait for low tide to uncover an area, then they dig with
a knife. The way I do it is to disregard high tide/low tide. I get into
the water and I dig with my hands. That permits me to feel whatever
I find. I can't see it because the water gets muddy. So I feel. And it's
great when you suddenly feel the shape of a mussel. It's like you sense
in the dark and you feel somebody's toe.
TF: It could be frightening to some people.
MIT: It could be (laughs) yes! It's muddy, you can find all sorts of
things.
TF: They're closed up when you find them?
MIT: They're closed up. If you leave them out of the water, every
so often they have this siphon and they eject water and they squeeze
themselves back into the mud. We cook them with a little oil, and

a bit of lemon. You heat them up, and they crack open, and you just eat them. They have beautiful buttons on them.

The *Fourth* picture contains one element of obsidian that I'm holding in my hand. It is a *core.* The core is what is left of a chunk of obsidian after you have chipped off the tools or the weapons that you wanted. The leftovers, the prehistoric garbage. So in the background is the prehistoric garbage stuff. In the foreground is this core that I keep. The core is proof that there was a workshop here. It was not simply that bits of obsidian were used here, and left, or forgotten, or lost. They were actually worked right in the area. And on the top right is an old oyster. The cup of one side of an oyster. The base is where this black spot is, which contains some malleable material that permits it to hinge with the top. Oysters are a specialty in that area. I can say I'm the only one who recognizes the danger, so I cannot protect the situation. There are very few oysters left. I have stopped, a few years now, I do not get any oysters out, because the place has to be replenished.

The *Fifth* picture is a slice of salt. You can see that it is quite cohesive, the little crystals are sticking to each other. I kind of dip my spread-out palm into the hole, and lift up a whole, full piece of salt. And then that breaks up into a dozen pieces, one of which is what we see here. The salt is big and grainy, it is not like the processed salt we find in table salt.

The *Sixth* picture is one foxy type of beast that I have found in that area. It had a long and fluffy tail. It's kind of disfigured because it was all dried out. There was no beast left. It was just the teeth, some skeleton and the fluffed tail. Most probably other beasts have eaten what was there to be eaten.

The *Seventh* is a bronze cast of a horn that was also found in the area. There are a number of found objects that I transform into sculptural objects. I get them cast, or I cast them myself. And then I work on them and they become part of performances, activities that have some ritual content. And these are triggered or go together with other material that is sent over through the mail art network, or it is used on special occasions, at some collective point in time, or when there is work to be done with models. That happens either in the deserted area or in an urban situation. So there is a lot of taking from the area, and a lot that has been brought back to the area from outside sources.

TF: I didn't know this was a cast . . . It's something that is very ancient and ritualistic, and yet at the same time you've modernized it, in a sense, or technologized it, by recreating it.

MIT: Yes, yes. There's a series of horns, and definitely a horn is something that I keep repeating. Every horn is a different shape. There are also other objects that I can recall, like the arm of a doll that can become part of a necklace, and then the heel of a ladies' shoe, the handle from a cup, contemporary bits and pieces that were found in some special situation, or with the intention of putting them back into

some ritual activity. So they always become part of an activity.

The *Eighth*, was a watch that I found. It was a working watch, and I did this performance which I wanted to note, to have the trace of the time that I did it. So I hit the watch with a rock at twelve o'clock, so it stuck there. This is an *Apotypomata* of that occasion. As you will see in this picture the rock is a kind of sculpted-out rock, in the sense that it has edges, little craters, elongated craters. So it is very difficult to walk there, with any kind of shoe. You have to have a situation that permits you to jump from rock to rock, because they're razor sharp.

The *Ninth* picture, like some of the others, is an edible found object. It has medical applicability. My father has — I think it's called prostate —

TF: Yes.

MIT: Okay. So. Three years ago we worked it out that instead of taking pills, he could use the leaves from a wild pear tree. So then I had to go out and find wild pear trees. They make little tiny pears, say of 2 cm. diameter, and they have plenty of thorns! So I have to avoid the thorns, and collect enough leaves for the whole year. So my mother boils the leaves, and my father has to drink it three times a day. And he stopped taking the pills. And the doctor says he is doing very well, but he won't believe that he's not taking the pills and he's taking leaves. There are the leaves I'm picking, from the same area.

The final picture, *Number Ten,* is one of my good models who had come over, and she is wearing one of these electronic pieces, together with a local material which is part of the crab exoskeleton. I put it all together and made this necklace. She is wearing also clothing that we had found. I find these clothes, and I chop them up, and they become more decorative rather than for morality reasons or for the weather. I guess you find this kind of clothing a lot in science fiction book covers. It's neither clothing to keep the woman fully clothed, nor to keep her warm.

TF: Covering, barely . . .

MIT: Barely! So this was also part of an activity, part of a performance.

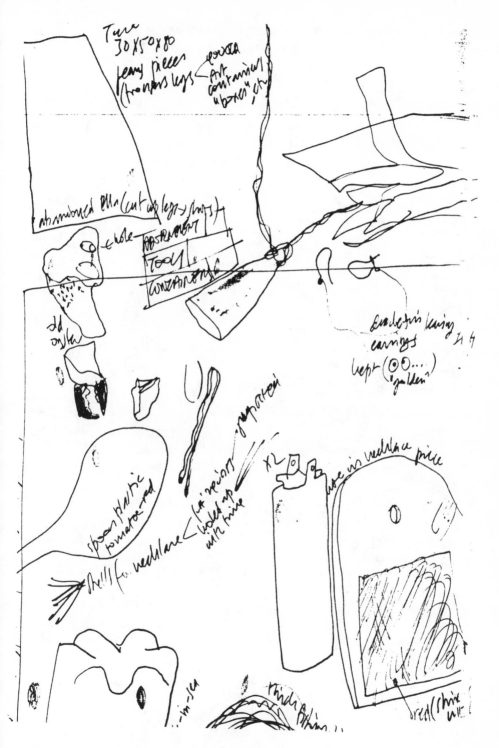

obsidian traces survived (see p17 summer persons and found winter times)

3/7 11 pieces (1 brown, ⬡)

97

(on the concave side)

Approaching Ella 29/6 /84

1.3   1.4

84

27/6

obsidian tool-making intervention

2 ceramics in tomb area

134

4/7 next to church Malion

2 ceramic (worked pieces, one with light brown color)

250

102

107

(really concave back (and

5/8 3 pieces, the possibly a stone.

7/8 9 pieces (⬡)

6/8 5 pieces (obviously two rejects from tool-making intervention)

Roihirbeach _ 4/8 4 pieces gone pretty

328

29-30/6 8 pieces (2 brown)

6/9 5 pieces

230

Mnila Αρχαιολογικα

QUESTION:

4/7 A bit of gray but pebbly stones even may Tiber opposite with watersanele.

4/8 one piece

1/8 7 pieces + one pebbly in Polmful itself

21/6 2 pieces (one brown, ⬡)

9/8 5 pieces (⬡)

ceramic base

27/6 Ansboheim 3 pieces ((tool-making ...

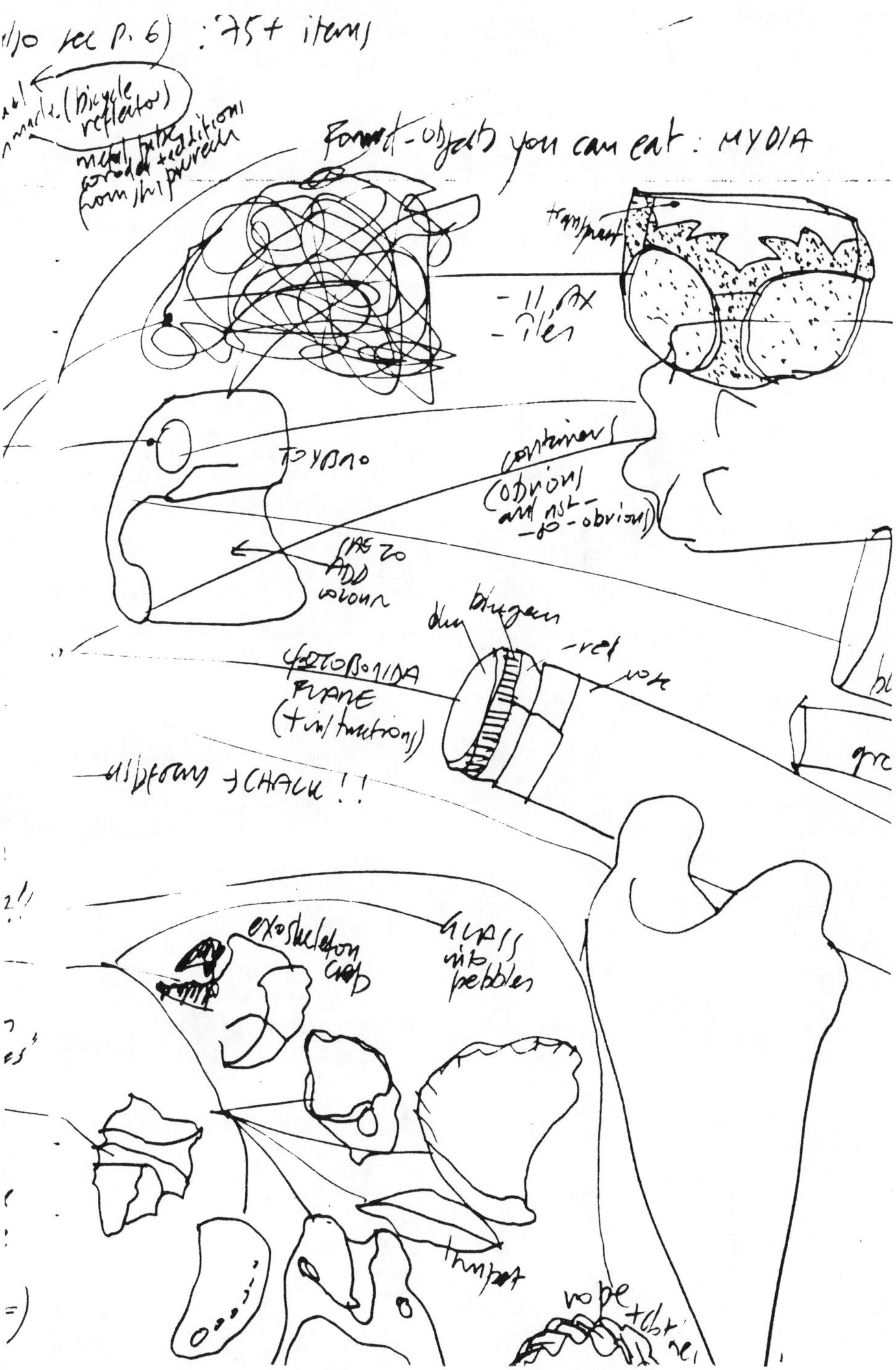

: 75+ items
(bicycle reflector)
objects you can eat
containers (obvious and not-so-obvious)
colour
bluegreen
red
CHALK !!
exoskeleton crab
glass with pebbles
trumpet
rope

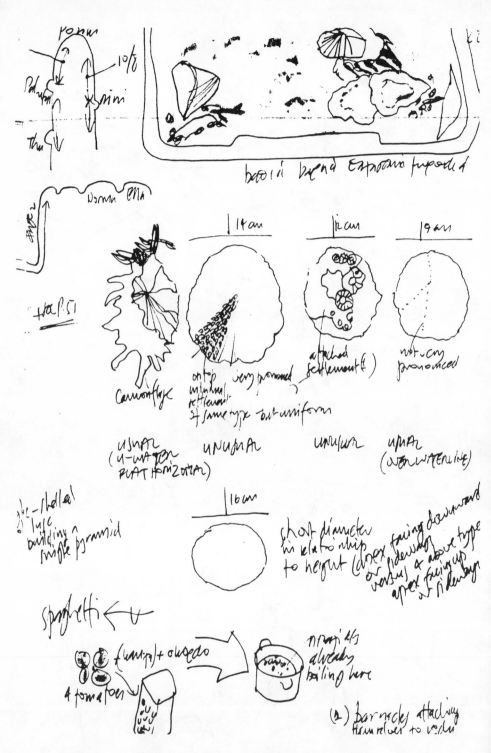

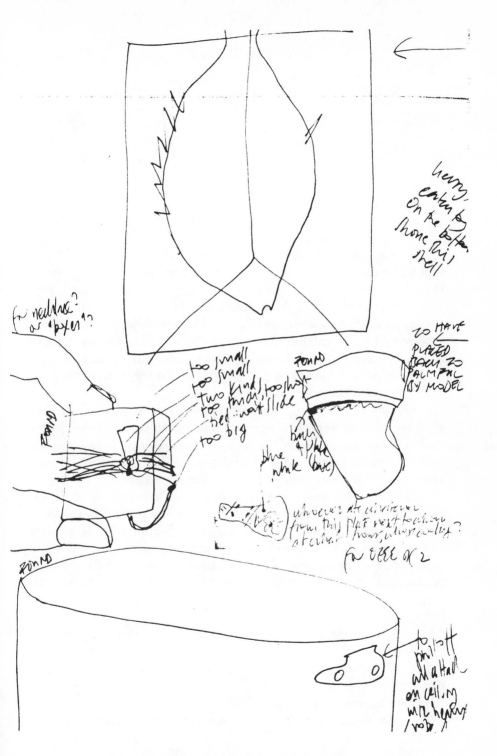

Richard LeMon

Conversation with a Geomancer

For a year I lived in Suzhou, an ancient city near Shanghai. Shortly after my arrival I became friends with a bright young man who taught at the same university as I. After a time I told him that I would very much like to speak with someone who knew about *feng shui* (wind water), the old system of Chinese geomancy which is used to site temples, houses and tombs. At the least, I hoped that my friend would put me in touch with someone from our History Department, someone who would most probably give me the Party's interpretation from an academic point of view. To my joy, five months later he had arranged an interview with Elder Wang Wei (not his real name) who has practised *feng shui* for fifty years.

Down one of Suzhou's narrow alleyways my friend and I walked until we came to a small two-story house, whitewashed below, weathered wood above, a gray tile roof. We were met by Wang Wei and led to the upstairs room: a wooden floor, an old Chinese table, three chairs, three teacups and a flickering kerosene light.

Elder Wang is seventy-three years old. He looks younger. He was wearing the usual garb of the day: blue pants and padded jacket, cloth shoes and a blue cap. This was the coldest February in forty years. Everytime we spoke, our breath rose in clouds. Elder Wang was smoking a long bamboo pipe with a brass bowl. I was told by my friend, who would act as interpretor, that we'd better not stay too long. After formalities, this:

RL: I want to thank you for taking the time to see me on this cold evening.
WW: Not at all. I'm always pleased to have guests. You're my first foreign guest, so this is my privilege.
RL: Is Suzhou your native home?
WW: Oh yes. I was born and raised in Suzhou. And I've lived in

this house for thirty-five years, half my life! I'm happy to live in Suzhou. It's a good place for a geomancer to be.

RL: I've thought that too. It seems that Suzhou is a very well-designed city.

WW: It is. Suzhou is a wonderful example of *feng shui*, not only because the city itself is laid out so according to principle, but because the gardens are as well. So, without, you have the strict *feng shui* principle, and within you have the gardens which recreate the natural world, again according to principle.

RL: Were the gardens laid out with the help of geomancers?

WW: Only the good ones! (laughs) The ones which have lasted. These couldn't have been sited without geomancers — they all worked hand in hand.

RL: Perhaps one day we could go to a garden and you could point out some of those principles to me.

WW: It's probably not best if we walked around together. I'm sorry.

RL: No, I quite understand. Forgive my asking.

WW: It's just that the authorities . . . well, dragons and tigers are fine for the foreign guests, but only on silk. (laughs)

RL: What makes Suzhou's *feng shui* so good?

WW: First of all, the watercourses running through the city. These allow the *ch'i* (energy) to circulate, like the veins of a man.

RL: Or like the *ch'i* meridians in acupuncture?

WW: Like those, exactly, except that the canals were man-made, so they could be planned. Then there are the pagodas.

RL: How do they work?

WW: In cities they serve the purpose of mountains, for protection against the wind and leaking *ch'i*. And they serve to gather and to focus the *ch'i*. For example, directly to the north we have the old nine story pagoda. This serves as our south facing mountain, which is usually necessary to a good site.

RL: I've often felt that Pan Men (a particularly old section of Suzhou in the southwest) seems special.

WW: Yes! That's because Suzhou has a very favorable northeast/southwest line of *ch'i* running through it. This follows the windcourses also. Have you noticed our west winds in Suzhou?

RL: They seem very . . . unfriendly?

WW: Unfriendly, yes! (laughs) But from the northeast come auspicious winds. What else about Pan Men?

RL: I don't know. What are you asking?

WW: What about the old pagoda?

RL: That's right! I always call it the Ghost Pagoda, because it's run-down and deserted.

WW: But it's not. It's very much at work, still gathering the *ch'i*. That's called the Auspicious Light Pagoda. It's part of the reason that Pan Men is so fortunate today. The *ch'i* pools there.

RL: How exactly does the pagoda work?

WW: Well, you just can't put anything up. All these new chimneys and smokestacks, you see, they're only clogging everything up. Mountains are the best protection and then after mountains, pagodas. Have you ever been in an airplane?

RL: Yes.

WW: That would be interesting.

RL: I wonder if we could talk a little about your early training. How did you become a geomancer?

WW: Yes, I was first taught by my grandfather who was a well known geomancer in Suzhou. He, in turn, had learned from his father. Our family has been one of geomancers for several generations. Upon the death of my grandfather I studied with my father. But that is curious.

RL: Why?

WW: Because, you see, at that time I had no idea that my father was a geomancer! I just thought that he ran our family store. Through the years he had also been learning from my grandfather, but privately, which is how it has to be. I never knew. He was just very secretive. Even more than I am now! So after my grandfather died I thought I was the boss. Then one day I was making some calculations for a gravesite and my father told me that he wanted to go along. So we went and I showed him the site. I was talking to him, you see, telling him all these things that I was sure he couldn't understand. Then my father, after he had listened to my reasoning, said, "Well, yes, you could put the tomb here, but that gingko is withering on the tiger's tail," which was just his way of showing me that the *chi'i* was seeping away and that the site was not so good. So then I listened to my father for another thirty years.

RL: What did he have to say?

WW: My grandfather was a master of the school of forms; that is, evaluating *ch'i* from the natural landscape formations. So the first thing we did was to take walks in the country. He would point out trees and rocks and mountains and show me how to tell which of the *wu hsing* (the five evolutive phases) they belonged to. Then we spent many times looking at the flow of watercourses, again looking at *ch'i*. Some days we would just go out and feel the wind. The wind, you see, dissipates the *ch'i*, so he would take me, say, to an eastern facing mountain and let me feel the wind, and then to a western facing mountain. And of course we spent many walks in the gardens in the city.

RL: Did he also teach you the compass?

WW: He did, yes, but my father taught me more. It wasn't that my grandfather didn't know it; he just didn't have time, enough years. And my father was more mathematically inclined, so he taught me most about the compass.

RL: What happened during the Cultural Revolution?

WW: Well, there was even humor there, because, of course, *feng shui* was outlawed and so I knew that the Red Guard would be around soon. So I divided my *feng shui* things into two piles: what they could have and what they couldn't have. I had many books then. Some of the books I left on my bookshelf. The remainder I hid, but not too well. So that they could find them.

RL: Why?

WW: So they would stop looking and leave. They were all useless books to me anyway because I had memorized them. So I hid them in my bed and they ripped open my bed and found them.

RL: And then they left?

WW: No. And then they searched for my compass, because they knew, because they were wise, that I must have one. So they ripped up a loose floorboard and found the compass.

RL: And so you lost that too.

WW: Yes, but that was the compass I had planned for them to find, so that they would leave. It was a relatively small compass, not so good. So then they left.

RL: And you had another compass?

WW: Another, yes. My grandfather's, which I hid here. (He unloosens a false bottom in the table and extracts a huge *feng shui* compass.) This is a forty-eight ring compass. I don't know how old it is. It was hidden right here, inside the table they were pounding on! (laughs)

RL: Do you have work now? *Feng shui* work, I mean?

WW: Before Liberation, I remember that we were asked to lay out a garden for a wealthy landowner. But we never did. And we were siting a lot of graves.

RL: Do you still do that?

WW: Yes, but only on the sly! (laughs) People still know what I do, but of course they're very quiet about it. Everyone knows, but no one knows.

RL: I suppose that the State has little use for *feng shui* now.

WW: Actually there is a great need, what with all the building. But you see the poor quality of it. Very little planning. The art is all here though, waiting, if they wish to employ it. It's all very old.

RL: Perhaps in the future.

WW: You will have to come back and ask my grandson about that.

Grady Clay

The Vietnam Veterans Memorial: Winners and Losers

For reasons that seldom get mentioned in the heat of aesthetic disputation—and certainly did not much figure in vituperations over the Vietnam Veterans Memorial in Washington, D.C.—any architectural competition can upset the status quo. It can exhume, even if it does not create, deep-seated myths and realities.

The notion that we should plan and pick and choose our environments—whether they be bicycle routes, housing projects, Court Houses or memorials—by means of an open, non-commercial competition held in full view of the public has been slow to catch on in the United States.

I will put forward the thesis that in a capitalistic, industrial society which prides itself on competition in business—sink-or-swim, compete-or-die, fight your way to the top—the notion of open competition, of results openly arrived at, has been, historically speaking, almost unheard of in the world of fine arts.

Why should this be so?

In the fine arts, the tradition of the patron is still pervasive and powerful—even in a society that claims to be egalitarian and is deeply pervaded by the populistic spirit. The royalist tradition continues, whereby rich and powerful individuals, who might be called the local Medici, control or seek to control the giving of favors, the awarding of commissions or contracts, the selection of artists. All of this in ways is quite reminiscent of Renaissance Italy and France. Even though one of our most famous public places—Central Park in New York City—was built to follow the design chosen in a formal competition in 1857, the very idea of aesthetic competition had to overcome many an obstacle.

Versions of this paper have been presented at Iowa State University and at The University of Kentucky.

And if one considers the way jobs and commissions still get shopped around, the way rich art patrons get hustled, and the highly personal deals thereby consummated, it is easy to conclude that the game is still played somewhat as it was when royal favors determined the choice of artist and subject-matter. The so-called competitions of those times were mere screening devices to placate the public while the real deals were concluded behind the scenery.

That could describe the conditions that continued pretty much up into the 1960s, when the idea got picked up in the United States that key tracts of land, proposed for urban redevelopment, should be sold or leased, not to the highest bidder, but to the bidder with the best new neighborhood design chosen by an impartial jury. This idea at first was highly suspect. It was looked down upon, like those early over-the-shoulder seat belts, as a fancy con game being foisted on the public. But it was an idea whose time had come.

The 1960s offered a fascinating testing-ground for the new competitions. Dozens of cities went in for the so-called developer competitions in order to choose the best plans and the best teams of designers and developers. Of the hundreds of projects coming out of that process, I would put the Golden Gateway in downtown San Francisco at the top, with Society Hill of Philadelphia a close second.[1]

What also emerged from that period beginning around 1965 was a hard core of hundreds of designers with the heady experience of forming teams to compete for big commissions, conspicuous locations and ownerships, and much publicity. Every wave of competitions became the testing ground for the next generation of hot-shots.

The preliminary skirmish occurred in 1961. Many architects, landscape architects and planners of the Sixties and Seventies had jumped into the Franklin Delano Roosevelt Memorial Competition in Washington. (That year, 1961, by the way, was the year of the first recorded death of an American serviceman in what we now call the Vietnam War.)

Scores of today's top names in the design professions entered that Roosevelt Memorial Competition. Two of the Roosevelt jury were to become members of the Vietnam Veterans Memorial jury twenty years later: Pietro Belluschi, then dean of architecture at MIT; and Hideo

---

[1] Clay, Grady. *The Competitors*, a study of developer competitions, The Joint Center for Urban Studies of MIT and Harvard, Cambridge, Mass. 01238, 1961. Unpublished monograph.

Sasaki, then head of landscape architecture at Harvard. The Roosevelt Memorial competitors included Charles Moore, Michael Graves and Richard Meier; Robert Venturi, Edward Larrabee Barnes, the Texas firm then Caudill Rowlett and Scott, Louis Kahn, Philip Johnson, Lawrence Halprin, Robert Zion, Robert Royston, and the late and famed teacher of landscape architecture, Stanley H. White, brother of the more famous writer, E. B. White.

Four of the Roosevelt Memorial competitors ended up as members of the jury for the Vietnam Veterans Memorial: Harry Weese, Garrett Eckbo, Hideo Sasaki, and Constantino Nivola.

The Roosevelt Memorial design chosen in 1962 suffered from critical review, by far the most serious coming from the Roosevelt family, still politically powerful; and reinforced by the wishes expressed by the late Franklin Roosevelt before his death. . . . It was never built. Instead, a new design, this one by Lawrence Halprin, of San Francisco, who was one of the 1961 competitors, was authorized in 1982 by Congress and the bill signed by President Reagan. It carries out at least one of the themes of the unbuilt winning design of 1961 — the so-called "Instant Stonehenge." Both the 1961 and 1982 designs call for large stone masses through which the walking public may proceed. But beyond those processional similarities, they are quite different.

Now to the Vietnam Veterans Memorial. Its specific start lay in the determination of a young U.S. Army veteran, Jan C. Scruggs, who returned wounded from Vietnam with shrapnel still in his body, and a resolve in his mind that those who fought in that war should get more than the scorn and disregard which greeted so many of them. He formed a committee of veterans, which later became the non-profit Vietnam Veterans Memorial Fund, or VVMF. He and his buddies got a bill introduced into the Congress to provide space for the Memorial in Washington. The Memorial itself would be built with private contributions. The bill went through Congress in 1980 without a dissenting vote.

The VVMF began fund-raising, and hired the well-known landscape architectural firm of EDAW, Inc. to analyze and compare ten possible sites in the Washington area. They recommended a two-acre site at the western end of Constitution Gardens, about three-quarters of a mile west of the Washington Monument, and a short walk from the Lincoln Memorial.

At this point, VVMF turned to the well-known architect and

author of the leading reference book on competitions. Paul Spreiregen of Washington. Spreiregen and the VVMF set out to pick what they called a "world-class jury." The eight members were Pietro Belluschi, architect, of Portland; Garrett Eckbo, landscape architect of San Francisco; Richard Hunt, sculptor of Chicago; Constantino Nivola, sculptor of East Hampton, New York; James Rosati, sculptor of New York; Hideo Sasaki, landscape architect of Berkeley, California; Harry Weese, architect of Chicago, and the author of this account, editor and author, of Louisville, Kentucky.

The VVMF decided, quite deliberately, NOT to appoint a Vietnam veteran to the jury, on the ground that other jurors would tend to treat any Vietnam veteran as a "representative" of all veterans, and would defer unduly to that person's preferences during the judging.

But before they could start, the Fund had to make a formal public statement of the purpose of the Memorial, as follows:

> The Purpose of the Vietnam Veterans Memorial is to recognize and honor those who served and died. It will provide a symbol of acknowledgement of the courage, sacrifice and devotion to duty of those who were among the nation's finest youth. Whether they served because of their belief in the war policy, their belief in the obligation to answer the call of their country, or their simple acquiescence in a course of events beyond their control, their service was no less honorable than that rendered by Americans in any previous war. The failure of the nation to honor them only extends the national tragedy of our involvement in Vietnam.

And then the statement continues:

> The memorial will make no political statement regarding the war or its conduct. It will transcend those issues. The hope is that the creation of the memorial will begin a healing process, a reconciliation of the grievous divisions wrought by the war. Through the memorial both supporters and opponents of the war may find a common ground for recognizing the sacrifice, heroism and loyalty which were also a part of the Vietnam experience. Through such recognition the nation will resolve its history fully. Then the Vietnam Veterans Memorial may also become a symbol of national unity, a focal point for remembering the war's dead, the veterans, and the lessons learned through a tragic experience.

Well, no matter how grand and even precise its purpose, any competition, to be a success, rests entirely and often precariously upon the formal, written published Program. In my view, the Program produced by the VVMF and Paul Spreiregen was the most comprehensive and accurate which I have ever examined, which is rather a large number.

Everybody who wanted to enter was required to register intent by December 29, 1980. Copies of the Competition Program were mailed out the next day to the 2,573 persons registered. About 180 individuals and teams submitted over 500 questions.

Some of those questions are revealing:

Question: Can you define what is meant by a "political statement"? (You will recall that the Program said "The Memorial will make no political statement regarding the war or its conduct.")

Answer: "For purposes of this competition, a political statement regarding the war is any comment on the rightness, wrongness, or motivation of U.S. policy in entering, conducting or withdrawing from the war."

Question: "Is the VVMF aware of the risk taken if all possible segments of American society are not included in the participation and definition of the Memorial?"

Answer: "Yes. This is one reason why the VVMF decided to have an open, anonymously juried competition to design the memorial. The number of competitors and the fact that they represent all fifty states and several U.S. territories as well as all walks of life testifies to the extent of participation in the process."

Question: (This was one of hundreds of quite technical inquiries): "Within the 4.25 acres do topographic changes count as part of the two acre memorial area?"

Answer: "Yes, topographic changes do count if, for example, land sculpting is a major element of your design; No if the topographic changes are moderate and not the primary element of your design. Use your judgment. Do not overwhelm the site."

After all questions were in, the VVMF consolidated questions and answers into one document, and mailed one copy to each person who had entered the competition. This process left no legitimate opening for any disgruntled competitor to claim, after the fact, that the program was flawed.

When the deadline passed, there were fourteen hundred and twenty-one entries, the largest number entered in any formal design competition in the history of the country. Less than half were by registered architects.

Between five p.m. and midnight March 31, 1981, one hundred and fifty last-minute entries squeezed in — an historic re-enactment of the old charrette routine in the great L'Ecole de Beaux Arts tradition. "With five minutes to go, there was one woman who had her design laid out in the parking lot, filling in the return address." (*Washington Post*, 7 May 1981).

Next came the judging. Each entry had to be mounted on thirty by forty-inch boards. No videotapes, no personal appearances, no pop-ups, no fold-outs, no scaled models. Flat. Thirty by Forty. Period.

By the time the VVMF got around to hiring a hall, it turned out they had to hire Aircraft Hangar Number 3 at Andrews Air Force base outside of Washington. By the time all the display panels were hung up at eye level from metal frames, they stretched for 1.3 miles up and down and up and down Hangar Number 3. The process was not helped when an Air Force pilot revved up his jet plane over in one corner of the hangar, and blew down the entire house-of-cards, which had to be set aright again.

Before the jury came to Washington that spring week in 1981, our professional advisor Paul Spreiregen went through all 1421 entries, grading them roughly into three groups: First, those that were so grotesque or otherwise appeared to violate the program that it was unlikely the jury would choose them. Second, those he considered of possibly superior merit. And the remainder were all in between. We were not, of course, bound by his preliminary sorting-out and I believe we all made a point of looking at each and every one.

We had only five days to wade through the 1421 entries and come out the other side with a public statement. When I was chosen chairman by the other jurymen, I wanted to allow plenty of time for debate, disagreement, comparison, and final selection. I was also determined to keep my own complete journal record of all our deliberations.

At this point, Hideo Sasaki should be singled out for special tribute . . . Of all the jurors, with the possible exception of Pietro Belluschi, Sasaki had the greatest amount of experience as juror, judge and adjudicator. He had been, for example, a member of the Federal Fine Arts Commission for many years.

Before we began looking at the entries, Sasaki suggested to me that we all sit down together, and carefully go over the Program, to fix it clearly in our minds. After the first day, he again suggested that each of us speak about our own possible preconceptions. "We should talk this out," he said, [because] we're operating on a very wide range of personal criteria." My journal reminds me that I confessed that my values were "uniqueness and clarity" and "how it feels to move through it." Belluschi said "There has to be some suggestion of the human tragedy." Richard Hunt stressed the need for "ease of entry."

For three days, we weeded out the worst, the most grotesque, the weak and the indecisive. Every night Spreiregen and his crew gathered the survivors for us to study the next day in greater detail.

By the fourth day we were down to twenty, with fifteen Honorable Mentions and the first, second and third prizewinners to be chosen. The prizes were, of course, not peanuts: first prize was $20,000 plus the right to oversee construction of the winning design. Second prize was $10,000, third prize $5,000. The sum of one thousand dollars went to each Honorable Mention.

We huddled on that fourth day in a group, all nine of us in front of each entry. Suddenly one of the jurors — I think it was Rosati — jabbed his finger over my shoulder pointing to one sketch and demanded "What's that?" And "that" turned out to be somebody's very clear personal initials, drawn on the paving blocks. This was a clear violation of the rule for anonymity. So that one was OUT.

Early on, I thought we would have difficulty awarding first prize. In the beginning I had seen little merit in the Maya Lin entry, with its vague and almost abstract drawings. But repeated inspection and discussion gradually made it clear that it was unique; there was a greatness in its deceptive simplicity that grew on us . . . We were unanimous in voting it first prize; it stood apart from all the rest in its contemplative eloquence. The morning of our final day, I got up at 5 a.m. in a Georgetown hotel room to type the first draft of our decision. We worried that the VVMF might not accept our choice. But as it turned out they accepted it with an enthusiasm diminished only by fear that the public might not "get" the full intent of Maya Lin's design . . . This was forestalled by three days of intensive and secret scale-model-building before the awards were announced, so VVMF could make the announcement with a comprehensible model to show off to the public.

The winner, Maya Lin, who was then an architectural student at Yale University, was the object of intense media scrutiny, tugged and hauled into talkshows, interviews and other intensities. Most of the early media coverage was favorable to neutral.

But of course winning was only the start of the debate. Within two months after our choice of the Maya Lin design, several Vietnam veterans, including two well-connected Washington lawyers, attacked the design. One criticism was justified and quickly remedied: in the original Lin design there was no specific inscription that paid tribute to the dead. The VVMF quickly agreed to add such an inscription.

But a small vocal minority, led by Tom Carhart and James Webb, the author of the well-respected book *Fields of Fire*, went public with accusatory words like "Orwellian glop . . . a black gash of shame . . . " and "a wailing wall for future anti-draft and anti-nuclear demonstrators" (Webb) and "a political statement of shame and dishonor" (Rep. Henry Hyde, Republican, in a complaint to President Reagan.)

The American Institute of Architects saw the Webb-Carhart campaign — for so it appeared to have become — as a direct challenge to the whole process of having a juried design competition. Suddenly, the design looked to be a kind of national Rohrshach test.

By that Fall, the few but effective critics of the design had convinced the Secretary of Interior James Watt that this was a national controversy, and that he better stall for time at least. So Watt, who controlled what happened on National Park land, withheld the building permit — right in the middle of the VVMF's fund-raising efforts. It had already raised over three million but needed seven million to finish the job — which included covering the very high costs of hustling private donations across the whole country.

But the critics didn't stop with Watt. They went after the jury with an undercover smear campaign. This included false allegations circulated privately around Washington to the effect that one of the jurymen had been "a communist," and that I had lied about my own military record in World War II and — so they falsely alleged — had not been wounded on the Anzio Beachhead. We consulted a famous libel lawyer. I telephoned Mr. James Webb who seemed to be involved with the rumor-mongering and suggested that he check his facts, and that if the false allegations continued to circulate, somebody was going to get the hell sued out of them. For one reason or another, the rumors soon stopped.

But not the opposition. Secretary of the Interior Watt let it be known to the VVMF that, unless they worked out a compromise with the objectors, he would deny them a building permit. This would have killed the Memorial financially, since VVMF was at that moment deep into its money-raising campaign . . .

So the VVMF officers attended what they expected to be a small private conference to "work things out." Instead, they found themselves surrounded by more than 40 angry veterans who had been flown into Washington by Mr. C. Ross Perot, the Texas computer millionaire.

Now one must understand that Mr. Perot had come into this from the beginning as a supporter. He had given $150,000 to help finance the competition. But he didn't like the Maya Lin design, and neither did some of his employees, who included a high percentage of Vietnam veterans. And he was out to stop it.

At that meeting, surrounded by angry shouting opponents of the design, with Secretary Watt's threat hanging over their heads, the VVMF were forced to compromise. They accepted, and agreed to actively support, the inclusion of an American flag somewhere above the Memorial Wall; and the inclusion of a combat-group statue. Perot and his crowd wanted the combat group stuck immediately in front of the apex or V-notch where the two walls come together.

Then there followed much tugging-and-hauling, back-room maneuvering. To make that long story short, the Fine Arts Commission, which has legal authority in such matters, accepted the additions, but required that the new flagpole stay well back from the apex of the walls, and required that the combat group be kept back some two hundred feet southwest of the memorial, close to the entrance. It was a reasonable compromise. The Lin walls, the original memorial design, were thus protected from the intrusion. So far as I know, none of the Jury has quarreled with that resolution, and even Maya Lin, who was deeply offended by the whole struggle, has accepted it in good grace. The money was raised, the wall built and finished on time.

Then on Veterans Day, November 11th, 1983, came the climax — the parade down Constitution Avenue, and the dedication, which went off with great emotion and no disruption.

The day beforehand, I was asked by *The Louisville Courier-Journal* to meet Maya Lin at National Airport, and escort her to the Memorial for photographs. We slowly wended our way through large groups of veterans. Some of them recognized Maya Lin and clustered around to shake her hand, to offer congratulations, many with tears in their eyes. Several said they'd had reservations about the design, but now endorsed it with emotion. But as we reached the apex at the center of the Memorial, suddenly, a tall young man, handsome, red-haired, wearing his Purple Heart, accosted Maya Lin and began shouting accusations. "WHY DID YOU DO SUCH A THING? THIS IS A MEMORIAL TO YOU, NOT TO US!" . . . He screamed and ranted, hardly giving her a chance to answer. She stood her ground, tried to speak. One photographer caught a picture of the three of us, with me, tape-recorder in hand, acting somewhat as an ineffective buffer. Finally three young men in green berets moved in on the screamer, told him to "cool it" and as he backed off, we left. Afterwards Maya Lin confessed that she'd gone back to her hotel and wept; it was the most personal and shattering confrontation she'd had. Up till then, the controversy had leveled off at a rather professional level — a debate among specialists. This was nasty and personal. But she is a strong person. There's a steel spring inside that small body, made tense by determination. And by a strong family history of Chinese teachers, artists, poets, and intellectuals.

What has happened since November 82 is now a familiar story and television scene — the touching visitations by thousands of veterans and families. They leave their flowers, they reach out and touch those names, they fall silent in the place, they seek help and comfort from those around them. This Memorial became in 1983 the second most heavily-visited tourist spot in Washington, next only to the White House.

How will it survive over time? What will be its power to reach out to future generations? In another 50 years there will be few widows and brothers or sisters still alive to make the pilgrimage. The children of veterans will come . . . for awhile. But as the survivors and memories fade away, then what?

I believe there is lasting power in those names. Yet even when that power diminishes, there is another force at work in this place . . . that mysterious force which earth itself and its configurations seem to possess, and to have exercised far back into pre-history. For this place is a man-made open valley, with the memorial walls along its north side. Once you descend its easy slope you are enclosed; it is suddenly quiet; traffic noise fades away; you are held in the visual embrace of nature.

Sometimes this force which lays its hold upon visitors is translated as "the spirit of the place," but that phrase has lately become a catchword, tarnished by advertising usage. Architects who have abandoned Le Corbusier and Mies and Gropius as their heroes now grope around for "contextualism" and come up with "the spirit of the place." The search for spirit-of-place has been an historic specialty within the profession of landscape architecture but now it became fair game for building architects and real estate ad salesmen.

But in spite of all that self-serving rubbish, we do seem to be in a new exploration. Some of this new uncovering is being done by hard-hearted and traditional scientists, who examine the phenomena in and of specific places—looking for electronic, acoustic, and other wave-generated phenomena. The Japanese and Chinese studies of ecomancy and geomancy explore aspects of "place" still foreign to most Westerners.

For us properly to appreciate the symbolism, those invisible but palpable feelings and impressions generated by these new shapes—not only by the Maya Lin design, but many many other landscape sculptures in this competition—we have to shift focus and consider the larger context within which most memorials occur. For our Western culture is building-bound. We create significance by enclosure—by putting a structure around it. We "save" a historic building—by enclosing it in a new Greek temple. Or Benjamin Franklin's non-existent house in Philadelphia by enclosing its disappeared reality with a space-frame.

The idea that an open landscape, or an open site such as the Vietnam Veterans Memorial, has significance of its own has been slow to get accepted in the United States. The idea that you can structure space and human experience by shaping earth and its components is still out-of-this-world. It is something primitive peoples did—and you know what happened to them!

We've become a people brainwashed by traditional architects to think of buildings rather than landscape as our special form of communication. And we have been long taught by economists that the highest and best use of open space land was to cut it up into saleable pieces of real estate, then cover it with buildings, and make money off of it.

The Vietnam Veterans Memorial Competition broke with this tradition, as did the Roosevelt Memorial Competition twenty years earlier back in 1961. The so-called "landscape solutions" seem to be winning in the end: the Maya Lin design has become tremendously popular; and the Lawrence Halprin memorial to Franklin Delano Roosevelt is in the design stage. Landscape art has gained a new acceptance, which was reflected in many of the Vietnam Memorial proposals. But that's not the whole story.

Competition consists of struggle. Aesthetic debate is hard-ball stuff and quickly turns into emotion if not violence. The same can be said of symbols. The deeper the meanings we attach to them, or allow to be released by them, the more likely we are to be shocked at the results. Beauty is, after all, more than skin deep. For lurking between the outer shape and colors of what we see and feel with our hands or bodies there lie unfathomable frontiers of experience, reaching back deep into our primordial past, and also exploring something of futures we have not yet experienced. A great work of art, even a memorial to something of the past, can uncover an emerging culture to which we had no pre-vious clue. In this case, Maya Lin's great wall solidified a phenome-non—the so-called landscape sculpture trend—which had been only episodically apparent, only sporadically accepted. I think it will resem-ble in its longterm impact Duchamp's famous "Nude Descending a Staircase" at the New York Armory show early in this century.

Works of art have indeed escaped from the art galleries. No longer must a work be designed, sized and shaped to go through museum doors for public exhibition, get sold, get hauled out those same doors and set up in another room at great cost. Great works of art, it is plain for all to see, can be a permanent part of the great outdoors. This process is a part of the de-structuralization of architecture. It speaks to a unification of the design process that may yet heal the split among the design professions. And that is something worth waiting and work-ing for.

There is something else to be said about this Memorial, and here I speak not so much as a jury member but as a Southerner who spent much of his life in that one region of the United States.

There is no way a Southerner who knows history can think about war exactly as do non-Southerners. For the Civil War was fought on our own territory, in our own places. My home town of Atlanta was that rare specimen—an American city burned to the ground by enemy action. General William Tecumseh Sherman, as they said, "was right smart of a general. But he was pretty damned careless with fire!"

And that was a war unarguably, undeniably and irrefutably lost. Many historians claim the South was a loser from the start. Not only was the Civil War fought over property rights to human beings—slaves—rights which were wrong morally and indefensible historically. But it was fought by the South from a shallow industrial base. THAT made successful war as unlikely and as difficult as was the waging of war in Vietnam halfway around the world.

In the Civil War, the South's enemy was, in fact, a great industrial nation with power which could be expressed by a new military weapon, the railroad. This was quickly perceived by the military powers of Europe, who sent more military observers to the Battle of Atlanta than had witnessed any battle in history.

In Vietnam, America's great enemy was distance and its costs, coupled with an implacable people defending their homeland . . . In Vietnam, the U.S. had no delivery system comparable to the American railroads of the 1860's. (And to talk about a delivery system for nuclear warheads offers us that most annihilating prospect of all — a nuclear war which puts an end to the very notion of prospects.)

The aftermath of the Civil War included occupation of the South by Union troops and politicians until thirteen years after Lee's surrender at Appamattox. And its economic and political effects have ricochetted up into our own time. The battle over civil rights in the 1960s continues a long struggle to free the South from many forms of slavery — economic as well as racial.

Southerners learned a unique lesson — how to live with the bitter taste of a war not won, a Cause not accepted by their countrymen; an economy not made whole for another century; and a tattered subculture scorned and disregarded for at least another hundred years.

Consequently, to have grown up in the American South between World Wars I and II was to have known — from first-hand evidence — what it costs to lose a war. For the South is a unique American region, filled with memorials to a lost cause, a lost war. At or near the center of any town or city of any pretensions to civic pride there is a Confederate Memorial, and even the most ignorant child of the South knows that it is meet and right and one's bounden duty to memorialize something other than a military triumph.

I say all this not to claim that Southerners were on the right side of the Vietnam War. Knowing what war is about, and looking at it from the unique position of the losers, gives a certain depth-perception to considering a war and its memorials.

A war fought and lost — however you define "losing," and for whatever reasons — is something most Americans, in contrast to most Southerners, never had to digest. And still, I think, barely begin to understand.

Since one of the most useless of all preoccupations is to continue fighting the last war, it is far better to learn your lessons quickly, and move on to face the future.

Consequently when I was asked to be a member of the jury for the Vietnam Memorial Competition, I hesitated not a moment. I was and am proud to have been a party to that transaction. I hoped that the competition would, in a way I could not then anticipate, begin the healing process to bring the nation together again.

"Together again" . . . My God, what a phrase to reckon with! The South of my youth still was a long way from becoming truly an integrated part of the American union, and it was easy for Southerners to feel the scorn of the majority. When I saw the treatment given Vietnam veterans as they tried to "rejoin the Union" of their own time, I was sore at heart. The least I could do was to help choose a memorial to be part of that healing process. That, I believe, is what this Memorial has begun to do.

Wichikapache and the Fish-heads

translated by Howard Norman
narrated by Joby Makinow

Wichikapache — this is about what happened when he caused trouble. He was in a village for a few days. He caused trouble there. He ate most of the fish the people there had caught. He left a few, only because they hid them. Mostly he left fish-heads, tails and bones. When he had eaten the fish, he began to leave.

"In which direction are you travelling?" an old woman said. She said in the middle of the village. She was gathering up fish heads, tails and bones. She was going to make a broth from them, a meal for the village.

"Easterly," Wichikapache said.

He set out.

Just as he reached the village-edge, the old woman said, "Well, good luck then on your travels, big brother. But I heard there was trouble in that direction. Hazards. I heard terrible rains had fallen recently. Many suckholes were made. People were falling in them. Well, good luck on your travel."

Wichikapache again set out, in the easterly direction. Soon he began having difficulty walking. He felt mud on his feet, but when he looked there was no mud! He walked some more. The mud-feeling was moving up. Now it was on his knees, and it was tougher going for Wichikapache. Then the mud-feeling was up to his neck! He began turning back to the village — the one he'd caused trouble in. The turning-around took him all day, because of the mud-feeling up to his neck! When he arrived at the village, he sat down. He was tired. Worn out by mud. He said, "WHO DO YOU THINK MADE MUD?"

No one in the village answered.

"Give me some broth!" he said.

"It's gone," the old woman said.

The next morning Wichikapache saw the old woman sitting in the middle of the village again.

"Hey, give me some food!" Wichikapache said.

"We don't have any," she said, "you took it."

With this, Wichikapache set out. He said, "I'm gone."

When he reached the village-edge, the old woman spoke up, "In which direction are you travelling?"

"Westerly," Wichikapache said.

"Well, good luck then in your travels," the old woman said. "Here, take along some food, why don't you." She tossed him some mouldy fish-heads. "Here, eat something. You'll need food on your travels!" Crunch, crunch, Wichikapache had something to eat.

But then the old woman said, "It's just that I heard that in the westerly direction ashes were caught in everyone's throat. Fires have been burning there. Big fires. There's coughing and ashes in the throat in that direction. That's what I heard. Well then, good luck in your travels."

Wichikapache set out in the westerly direction. Soon he began to cough. He was very thirsty. He drank some water, but it didn't help. He began to choke. Then he coughed some ashes out. Then he vomited up some ashes, a pile of them . . . it looked as if a small camp-fire had been rained on. It was wet black. Coughing. Coughing. Coughing. Wichikapache returned to the village. When he got there it was dark.

"Try and stop coughing," the old woman said. "We have people asleep here!" Cough, cough, cough. Wichikapache kept coughing. Finally he fell asleep, coughing in his sleep too.

In the morning Wichikapache was shouting, "WHO DO YOU THINK MADE ASHES? WHO DO YOU THINK MADE THE DIRECTIONS? I'VE WALKED NORTH, SOUTH, EAST, WEST MANY TIMES."

Then he set out.

"In which direction are you travelling?" the old woman spoke up.

"Southerly."

"Good luck then in your travels," she said. "Here, take along some food." Again she tossed him some mouldy fish-heads. "You'll need some food for your travels." Crunch, crunch, Wichikapache was very hungry. Crunch, crunch, he had something to eat.

He set out in the southerly direction, but when he reached the village-edge, the old woman said, "While you were asleep I heard about something."

"Is it about the southerly direction?"

"Yes," she said. "I heard that the close-eye sleet was living there. I heard that if a traveller comes along, it throws against the traveller. Sleet throws against the traveller there. It closes-up a traveller's eyes. It hurts your eyes and face. You can't fight it. It takes your eyes if it wants to. Sometimes. Sometimes it gives them back, but for days you still see sleet in them. That's the thing I heard."

With this, Wichikapache quickly turned around and set out in the *northerly* direction! "I'm gone," he said. "North."

He fled the village.

He was walking and soon he came to a sleeting place. It was sleeting and Wichikapache was having great difficulty seeing. He held still. The sleet threw at his face. "WHO DO YOU THINK MADE SLEET?" he shouted. He closed his eyes. "Listen, listen sleet! Stop throwing at me!" But — the sleet is so loud it can't hear anything!

"BUT I'M WALKING IN THE NORTHERLY DIRECTION! WHAT ARE YOU DOING HERE, SLEET?" But the sleet just threw itself at Wichikapache harder and harder. He covered his eyes.

His hands were cupped over his eyes, and he saw many things in the dark.

Finally the sleet left. Wichikapache returned to the village. There he shouted, "YOU LIED TO ME. YOU SAID THE SLEET WAS IN THE SOUTHERLY DIRECTION. BUT IT WAS NORTH." He shouted this at the old woman.

The old woman turned into a fish-head. Then Wichikapache saw that everyone in the village was a fish-head, fish bones or a fish tail!

"Awgh! Awgh! No, no! . . . " Wichikapache covered his eyes with his hands, but in the dark he saw the sleet again! He uncovered his eyes. He ran in the southerly direction. As he reached the village-edge, all the fish-heads spoke up, "In which direction are you going?"

"Southerly."

"Well, good luck in your travels," the fish-head village said. "We will meet you there!"

"Awgh! No, no . . . "

"Well, then, bring us fish-bodies, for we are just mouldy fish-heads, fish bones and fish tails!"

With this, Wichikapache said, "WHO DO YOU THINK MADE FISH?"

He put fish bodies on the bones, between the fish heads and tails. Then they turned into the people of the village again. But the fish remained too! So there were many fish to eat.

They began eating, but Wichikapache was gone! That's what happened.

Wichikapache and the Rain-huddled Girl

translated by Howard Norman
narrated by Samson Autao

There was a man and his wife, and when they had a child she couldn't resist rain. Whenever it rained, she'd walk out to stand in it.

"Didn't you know it was raining?"

She wouldn't answer. She stood in the rain. Inside her house, people sat and talked and they could see her. They kept the door open to look. Her parents loved her; she grew to be beautiful. Yet it was true that, because she so often stood in the rain, that her own mother dreamed of ringing out her daughter's clothes again and again.

One day, people looked out and there she was. She was standing rain-huddled, but it was clear out! Sunny. She was standing rain-huddled though. People saw this.

"Maybe she knows rain is coming, and she's getting ready for it," someone said.

"No, it's clear out. It won't rain for days."

Then something was heard in the bush near the village. The people ran over and saw a moose tromping through the bush.

Then the girl went in her house and sat down.

"Surely this is her undoing!" her mother said. "She mistook the moose-sound for rain!"

That night the girl could not sleep, and her parents could not sleep either because they were watching her. Her mother prepared some food. She cut up pieces of a moose and prepared it. Soon everyone in the village was there, eating. The girl lay in the corner, not sleeping. They tried feeding her bits of moose, but she refused. "I don't eat rain, I stand in it," she said. They tried to get her to eat some bits of moose again, and again she refused.

Presently she stood up, and stood near the door. It was dawn, and it was going to be a clear day. Everyone was yawning from being awake all night. Even with their eyes half-closed with yawns they still could see it was going to be a clear day. Then the girl stood outside, rain-huddled. She looked at the sky. Then she looked at the ground. Then she took off her jacket and wrung it out. No rain dripped out of it, though, as far as the people could see. The girl put the jacket back on.

"This surely is her undoing!" her mother said. "Just look how she's standing in the sun, rain-huddled! This surely is her undoing!"

Just then they heard a noise in the bush, near the village. They ran to look. There they saw a lynx with its head turned back at them, but its body leaning the other way. It held still that way a moment, then fled. It ran and was gone. The faster it ran, the tighter the girl held herself . . . to her, the lynx running made it rain faster. When the lynx was out of sight, the girl went into her house. Immediately she went to the corner. Again all night she stayed awake. The other people stayed awake too. In the middle of the night her mother began preparing a lynx to eat. She split the skin — on the inside hind legs — from the paws to the vent. She tied the hind legs together, then hung the lynx over a tree limb and skinned the rest. Then she folded the fur off, inside-out. She melted some fat and made a stew. Everyone ate, but when some was offered to the girl she refused it. "I stand in the rain, I don't eat it," she said. The people ate the lynx stew. The girl wouldn't eat any. They all stayed awake with each other. She lay in the corner, waiting for the next day's rain.

The next morning she stood outside. She waited until some fog left, and the sun came out; then she stood rain-huddled.

"She's rain-huddled!" her mother said. "What can we do?"

Presently Wichikapache arrived and began telling things. He said, "In the next village to the East of here, where I recently was, I was causing all sorts of weather. Storms, lightning, thunder." Wichikapache was bragging about the weather he'd caused. This was Wichikapache, who did nothing but travel between villages. Sometimes he was called Who-Travels-Between-Villages. He knew about weather in villages and between villages. He'd caused some. He'd seen all kinds of rain as well, and had himself stood rain-huddled — when he got caught in the very rain he'd caused! Things such as this happened with him. But the present morning he arrived, it was clear and sunny, and he was not standing rain-huddled. He stood near the girl; one was rain-huddled, one was not — both under the sun!

Wichikapache continued his talking: "Now, here in this village, I'm going to do many things with weather! Already I've made a moose sound to this girl as rain, and a lynx-growl sound to her as rain as well! If I want to, I'll do this with all the animals! IF I WANT TO

I WILL!"

Then Wichikapache said, "I'll start with otter-rain, go on to beaver-rain, caribou-rain. . . . each morning another rain-sound, and each morning, in the sun, this girl will stand rain-huddled!"

That's what Wichikapache said.

"We won't get *any* sleep!" someone shouted. "We'll have to stay awake with this girl, trying to get her to eat something. We'll have to be cooking all night. We'll become night people!"

Now all this was becoming intolerable to the people there, so what happened next was this:

The rain-huddled girl saw that Wichikapache was using her to deprive her village of sleep. Everyone was very tired; nothing was getting done, except for the staying awake at night! She knew she had to do something. So: even though Wichikapache was trying to keep her standing in different rain-sounds in the sun, she suddenly walked right into her house!

Wichikapache was made very angry by this. He made a nearby otter sound as rain. He made a nearby beaver sound as rain. He made a nearby caribou sound as rain.

But inside her house, the girl was unravelling herself from all the days she'd stood rain-huddled. She was spinning in circles. Watching this — through the open door — Wichikapache got dizzy and he fell over!

"Now I'm very hungry!" the girl shouted. Then she began eating the stews made from the animals Wichikapache made sound as rain. Hunters from her village had gotten them.

"Not too much water in those stews!" she shouted.

With this, Wichikapache got up from the ground and began walking toward the next village.

That's how the rain-huddled girl sent him away.

Wichikapache Steals Language

translated by Howard Norman

Wichikapache hadn't caused trouble in a few days. He went walking. He said, "I'm going to the first village I ever made." He was talking about a time, long ago, when he walked around starting villages. Duck villages. Wolf villages. Crow villages. Animals scattered out from these villages. Then he started human villages, too. Wichikapache started those! Wichikapache knew about the origin of many things. But he also brag-lied. He twisted stories around, if he wanted something. Sometimes his tricks worked, sometimes they didn't. Yet no matter what he did, Wichikapache ended up setting out again alone. Walking. And the time I'm telling about here, Wichikapache said, "I'm going to that village of humans. I'll tell them who made their village. I'll tell them who made the world. They'll take good care of me there . . . "

As he neared the village, Wichikapache smelled fish and heard scale-scraping; noises of fish out of water. Then he heard an old woman say, "This pickerel had a bad temper. He bit at reeds. He chased himself," she laughed. Wichikapache walked closer, to watch. The old woman scraped the scales from the fish. Then she cut it open and took out its insides. Up in a tree, a crow asked for the insides of the fish. The crow said, "Give me those insides and I'll tell you what I see from up here . . . " The old woman tossed the fish insides on the ground, and the crow swooped down and ate them. Then the crow said, "From in my tree I saw fish insides being tossed to the ground Awwwgh, Cawwwgh!"

Whenever a crow came around, humans got some practice in being tricked. But the old woman tricked back, "Crow — you know what I saw in those fish insides?"

"What?" the crow said.

"No, first you tell me if Wichikapache is around here. Then I'll tell you what I saw in those fish insides."

The crow flew from tree to tree. The crow circled the village, then landed again. "No, Wichikapache isn't around," the crow told the old woman.

"Then who's standing just at the edge of our village?" she said.

With that, the crow flew. But the crow had to worry what was in those fish insides! The crow worried the whole day about this.

The old woman went on cleaning fish. Wichikapache still hid in the trees. The old woman said, "This pickerel," — she held it very still, in the air — "could hold still in the fastest of currents . . . " Then she scraped that fish. She cut it open and tossed its insides on the ground, but the crow didn't take them. Then the old woman held a pickerel away from her. She said, "This one has many scars from fighting. This one liked to fight." She scraped that fish too. She had a good memory, from what she was taught and from what she saw. Many women were cleaning fish, and she was talking about the fish lives. "Pickerel have difficult lives," she said, "but they can have good lives too." She talked about pickerel.

Just then Wichikapache shouted, "WHO DO YOU THINK MADE PICKEREL? WHO DO YOU THINK MADE THE WORLD?"

Nobody looked up. They just went on cleaning fish. The old woman said, "The edge of the village is talking again."

"IT'S ME SHOUTING! WICHIKAPACHE!"

The women just went on cleaning fish.

The old woman said, "There's still a very old pickerel in the lake," she wrinkled her face, "so old, old, old. And so smart about life, it even forgot how to be caught. Doesn't even think about that! So old, it's learned to nab a whole day from the top of the water — just before the day sinks into the lake. Old. Old. I'm thinking this pickerel made the world," she said. She didn't look over at Wichikapache.

Hearing all this, Wichikapache grew angry. He shouted, "I MADE THE WORLD!"

The old woman leaned over to listen, at a fish. "I hear someone shouting. Is it you, fish?"

More angry, Wichikapache stood right in front of the old woman. "I'M HERE!"

Finally the old woman looked up from the fish. She said, "Are *you* Wichikapache? I can't remember."

More angry, Wichikapache said, "Can't you see who it is? CAN'T YOU REMEMBER? I MADE YOUR VILLAGE! I TAUGHT YOU TO

CLEAN FISH!"

The old woman looked back to the fish. "I'm sorry, fish," she said, shaking her head, "I planned to remember things about you fish today. But now it seems I'll have to remember something else . . . "

Then she said to Wichikapache, "Well, I'm still not sure it's really you. I'll have to ask old Two Loons. She'll know. She has the best memory of anyone."

"I HAVE THE BEST MEMORY!"

"Now I remember something else," the woman said. "I remember that Two Loons has a better memory than Wichikapache. A better memory than you, Wichikapache, who has none! If that's who you really are!"

All this made Wichikapache even more angry.

The old woman walked Wichikapache to a lake. Wichikapache just followed her. Whenever an old woman walked to a lake, Wichikapache followed even though he never knew what would happen there. On the lake shore, the old woman shouted, "Two Loons! . . . "

"Two Loons! . . . Two Loons!" the lake shouted back.

This was a lake that doubled every shout.

She dove into the lake. She disappeared under the water. Soon she flew out and stood in front of Wichikapache. She was dripping wet. She said, "I am Two Loons. But I had to dive into this lake to remember that. I have the best memory, after I dive into this lake."

Then Wichikapache felt water dripping from himself, too. "WHO DID THIS TO ME?", he pointed to the water dripping from him. "WHO DID THIS TO ME?"

Wichikapache was confused. Wichikapache was puzzled by this, but still he said, "I knew that! WHO DO YOU THINK MADE THIS LAKE?" He bragged.

Wichikapache bragged but Two Loons was already walking away from him, toward the village. Then she flew there. Wichikapache followed her.

When they arrived in the village, Wichikapache gathered everyone together. Everyone was supposed to look at him.

Then Wichikapache turned into a deer.

Wichikapache asked Two Loons, "What is my name?"

Two Loons said, "*Utiwaswun*" — deer horns.

Then worry was on everyone's faces. Two Loons noticed this.

Two Loons tried again, "Your name is *Utiwastise* . . . " — deer's sinew.

Someone said, "Two Loons can't remember the word!"

Two Loons grew frightened and began calling out, "Deer-eyes, deer voice, deer hooves!" But none of these worked.

Wichikapache then said, "I'm making it so you — Two Loons — are the only one who can call DEER in close. So if you can't remember how to say DEER, all the DEER will be insulted and leave, and there will be no DEER to eat!"

Two Loons flew back to the lake, and Wichikapache followed. She dove in, and swam on the lake awhile. She flew out and landed back in the village. Soon after Wichikapache arrived. There Two Loons began to sing:

> You   who stands sideways
> looking at us
>
> You   who flick your tail
> up
>
> You   whose fawn is covered
> with dew

Her song went on, and it had many deer in it, and the things you always see deer doing.

The deer were listening. They heard that Two Loons knew many things about them, and they were pleased with this. The deer walked into the village.

"They're giving themselves up!" someone said.

When this was said, many more deer appeared next to the lake. Some were killed and stored for food and some were eaten right away. Seeing the deer being killed frightened Wichikapache, so he changed back to his old self, just in time!

Two Loons said, "Yes, that must be Wichikapache, who remembered to change back in time! Ha! — he's no longer a DEER." There was much laughing.

This laughing sent Wichikapache out of the village. He went walking.

He walked and walked, and he couldn't find anything to eat. "I'll find something in a dream!" he said. Then he fell asleep. It became night. During the night, Wichikapache turned over in his sleep. He turned again. Then he turned another way, all during his sleeping. When he woke, he said, "In which direction was I walking?" He'd forgotten.

His sleep-turning got him lost. He set out again. He walked and walked. He said, "That dream didn't bring me any food!"

After awhile Wichikapache smelled something. Venison! He walked to a village-edge. In the village he saw people preparing a deer to eat. This made him call out, "I'M HUNGRY!"

No one looked up from the deer. Wichikapache shouted, "WHO DO YOU THINK MADE DEER?"

Just then Two Loons landed on Wichikapache's head. He was back in the same village! Two Loons said, "Why should we give you food? You tried not to let us eat deer!"

"Did I do that?" Wichikapache said. "Did I do that?"

Then a villager tossed Wichikapache some antlers. Another tossed him some deer's sinew. Another tossed him some deer hooves. Wichikapache begged for venison . . .

They went on cleaning the deer.

Wichikapache threw himself to the ground. He groaned. He groaned and cried. He tied the antlers to his own head. He tied the deer hooves to his own feet. He begged for venison again.

Finally they gave Wichikapache some venison to eat.

Wichikapache can't change though! He tried to get more. He tried to gobble the whole deer! But the villagers wouldn't let him. They sent him walking. He went walking, but right away his antlers got stuck in some low branches. He tripped and fell over, and the groaning and crying started up for real then. He got up but fell again, because he couldn't walk on those hooves. Finally he took them off, the hooves and antlers.

He went walking.

Narrated by Samuel Grey Sturgeon
Kiskito Lake, Manitoba

Alex Shoumatoff

from The Ituri Forest

Gamaembi picked some white-gilled mushrooms with light-gray caps and foot-long taproots. He said they were called *imamburama* and were good to eat. That evening we ate them sauteed in *mafuta* with rice and sardines, and they were good. We would sleep on *mangungu* pallets in a lean-to on the Afande River which two men from Opoku had recently built as a fishing and trapping camp. After supper, I tried one of Baudouin's joints. The *bangi* was very smooth and relaxing, but it wasn't conducive to clear thought, and when I got up to poke the fire back to life I discovered that it made tedious demands on motor coordination. Gamaembi didn't touch the stuff. "For me, life is already wonderful," he explained.

He and Baudouin were fascinated by the color plates in Jean Dorst and Pierre Dandelot's "Field Guide to the Larger Mammals of Africa," which we pored over with a flashlight. I wrote down the Swahili and KiLese names of the animals they recognized. I asked about leopards. Gamaembi said that a day in from the road they were quite common — especially along rivers. "We can hear him sing, cry, *etre dans la folie pour rien*, purr happily after killing an antelope," he said. He told me that you could hit a giant forest hog with a hundred arrows before it died, but that with a spear it only took once or twice. I asked about butterflies. The BaLese have many names for bees, but for butterflies they use only the general Swahili word, *kipepeo*. "Butterflies are bad for us, because we have no use for them," Gamaembi said.

"To me, the butterfly is the insect that climbs trees and eats the leaves," Baudouin remarked.

"Butterflies are metamorphoses," Gamaembi said. "We eat the caterpillars but not the butterflies."

"I love the forest, monsieur," Gamaembi said a little later, as we lay in the darkness. "To know its situation, to find all the marvellous little things and the mountains in it."

*   *   *

The *capita* of Zalondi told Gamaembi of a village that had been started since his last visit. It was up the Mubilinga River, and we could go to it instead of to three villages that Gamaembi was already familiar with. I said it sounded like a good idea. When we were back in the forest, I asked to go first, so I could learn to find the way. The path was well worn and about a foot wide — twice as wide as an Amazonian footpath, because the Indians put one foot directly in front of the other as they lope along. Sometimes it had lots of little offshoots. It wasn't easy to tell the ones that were shortcuts from the animal trails that petered out into nothing. The elephant trails, which crossed the path from time to time and sometimes followed it for a stretch, were deep and especially confusing. Sometimes the path would split in two, which meant that up ahead a tree had fallen across the original route. You took the newer-looking detour. Snapped saplings always meant something — usually that someone had rights to a nearby honey tree. Once, we came across a message carved on a tree in Swahili. It said, according to Gamaembi:

> I came by here in December, when you had gone in search of honey. Bring me some quickly.
> Sekufi

In time, I learned to let my feet make the decisions, and they were usually right.

Edwin Wilmsen

from Journeys with Flies

Entries

Thirsty. Thirsting skin flayed by sun and summer winds hot and dry
in this desert. Sand driven into nerves ground raw.

A tiny shortbed Landrover that looked like a wornout toy: for seventy-
five dollars its owner unloaded his cargo destined for a trader's store
to make the 160km side-trip westward to Kaikai where he left me under
a tree in the dark, soon surrounded by people who made a fire for
me and uttered not a single word that I recognized although they never
stopped talking.

August: beginning of the hot season when accumulated wrongs — of
the passed year, of the more distant past that had belonged to dead
grandparents, spouse's relations — are added together in shouted rage,
shored up sometimes by threats of bodily harm that one cannot be
certain will not be inflicted . . .

A few days after my arrival: two   1
men, second cousins, at each oth-
ers' throats

   i'll put an arrow in him when   2
   he's out alone in the bush   he
   promised my mother two birds
   she let him set snares around her
   dried-up cornfield   now he's eating all the birds he gets   now
   my mother is dying of hunger
   there is no food

   i'll get him at night when he's
   asleep and no one sees he made

incestuous remarks to my wife
his father always did that to
my mother who was his niece
saying things like i'll pull your
long labia things like that you
shouldn't say to people you can't
marry   i don't get many birds

Open threats, made public so they
will not need to be acted upon;
bound up tensions released . . .

Where the heat becomes too intense it must be vented upwards to
escape in swirling pipes created by its own velocity into a sky cloudless
for months.

In September, these dustdevils, like miniature tornados, rush through
the thornbush every day, big ones with a rough grating roar, small
ones with a sibilant swish; later, in October or November, two or three
may be seen in a single field of vision with a thunderstorm pouring
rain on another spot at the rate of an inch per hour.

At a distance, hidden behind the hump of a dune, their sound can
mimic that of a truck engine

a tow is coming   3

followed by speculation that it is the sound of a Landrover, or Toyota,
Ford, or 5-ton Bedford. But no vehicle appears.

Two weeks after I came to Kaikai: my first walk alone into the bush —
not a courageous move, following the well-marked vehicle spoor leading eastward toward towns and stores and showerbaths. I had been
delivered on this same road. Parting, my companions had said they
would join me within two weeks, after their tenth-hand truck was re-
paired (an acquaintance had told us this vehicle was an unwise choice,
but we knew he was not wise so ignored the valuable part of his experience); that time was now past, as it turned out another month would
go by before I saw them again. While I learned through many repetitions to pronounce in Zhu a tow is coming, but not to distinguish a
vehicle from the wind;

alternating between a desire to see my friends and being grateful for the chance to enter into this place free of their encumbrance . . .

There were three of us in the beginning, but in my memory I am alone. We each had our own motives for coming to this remote corner of the Kalahari and our own interests couched in terms of scientific models and hypotheses of social behavior. The same coordinates described our location but the contours of the space that each of us entered were different even before we arrived in Botwana in August 1973. And, in fact, through a series of unplanned events that kept my companions at a distance, I was alone for the greater part of the next six months—as alone as one can be with 160 Zhu of all ages, more or less, and 35 Herero, also coming and going, around the single set of open wells that held the only water for us all . . .

4

Walking in this loose sand will take some learning; pushing off from toes only makes my foot slide backwards producing a lot of sweat but little forward motion . . .

no motion at all last year to the day exactly leaning into the wind trying to cross Arapahoe glacier and climb the peak with Carl and Lisa making no headway against the gale almost blown over when we turned to go back beginning then to make the plans that brought me here already telling them that if it worked out I wanted them to join me for a time realizing that more than a new language would have to be learned but not that ordinary things like walking would be different . . .

Time to be bolder now, learn to navigate through the bush—more dense here than around the wells and camps where wood is cut for fences and firewood, to open a space for cattle management, and to eliminate shelter for snakes. Can't see more than ten feet in any direction; shouldn't become irreparably lost, haven't come more than a mile although I've been gone an hour stopping to watch birds, study leaves, beginning to feel the texture of this landscape: cowpaths crisscross in all directions where cattle browse, easy to see they prefer acacias to broad-leafs; follow the deep well-worn paths, they should take me back. Sitting on the tip of a twelve-foot termite hill everything looks the same, in every direction scraggly bushtops; the sun directly overhead projects no helpful shadows, wind still from the southwest so this should be the way — unless the wind has shifted and that isn't southwest . . .

> hanging onto the leader of a jackpine trying to see over the uniform tops of thousands of identical trees after a night snowstorm had obliterated all traces of trails . . .

but there downhill is unquestionably the way to go, here there are plenty of questions.

A few days later, far out in the bush with Twi, my namegiver-grandfather, and Tjitjo and Damo, they ask where is Kaikai and correct the point of my finger by three maybe five degrees laughingly saying I'll have to do better after I congratulate myself on being so close — my turn will come three years later in Gaborone when at the hotel I ask them to point to the center of town they say we don't know this place; Damo perpetuates the joke in January '80 when again in Gaborone Ssao points in diametrically the wrong direction to Kaikai and we recount stories of learning local geography.   5

I didn't particularly notice the young kid among the six or eight men who settled around the fire next to my tent early every morning to drink coffee before the sun was high and hot when we all moved under the shade of a huge acacia tree of the kind called camelthorn which Livingstone in his zeal thought must have furnished the wood for Noah's ark but really is most useful for dropping its big seed pods eaten by cattle when grass is thin in order to first create and then consolidate my beginning understanding of Zhu

in those days and for some time
thereafter I would tell people I spoke

broken Bushman babytalk but felt
secret satisfaction with my babytalk when ten weeks after arriving
I found myself one night 40km a-
way with no companion other than
Maitso whom I didn't know very
well at the time and was able to
make myself understood to total
strangers

but Damo was always there unobtrusive yet more often than not lying closer rather than farther from me in the sand taking his turn pro-
nouncing a word or offering a construction running in response to
the call "Daamuu" shouted by Katja or Maka the women of the Herero
family with whom his family had long been allied slipping back into
his place when the errand was done laughing when Twi taught me
to say I want you . . .

after a momentary flicker of embarrassment the three of us laughed too
when I fell over soft unexpected forms
on my way to pee out of the hemisphere of dancing cooking firelight
in the third clouddark night of my
Christmas party 75 as I sprawled
with my head propped on my arm
against Damo lying with Tabo still
vivacious and desirable a young wi-
dow with two small kids she died a
year later but at that moment I com-
plimented their choice of a bed in
the comparative seclusion of
my shallow excavations into   6
their recent history Damo
telling me in those days that he would
marry Ku but still had not worked
out the end of his affair with Tabo
while Ku clarified for me the particular kind of scoundrel he was since
everybody knew that Damo would
marry Ku and four years later have

their third baby in her belly the first
miscarried Kada nearly two now
staying with his mother's older-sister
in their father's camp to be weaned
loving the cheese and candy we bring
to him from our trips to Maun . . .

It seems impossible that six weeks
after that first timid excursion I set
out alone at dusk walking the
eight kilometers to the hill camp
to sleep there in order to leave before dawn on a kudu hunt with
Kumsa having convinced him that
my compass could guide me back
should I become separated from
him but not mentioning that in order to set a compass course the
starting point must be known and
because of that I won't bother to
bring the compass next morning
after several hours scanning we
pick up fresh spoor and run along
it closing the gap to a big male
kudu which I never reach my glasses opaque with sweat I tripped on
a fallen tree I didn't see and watch
Kumsa go on — then find my way
back to his camp deserted at mid-
day while everyone is out gathering food and on to Kaikai.

No one is surprised . . .

I lost 4 kilos that day   all water sweated out in the heat
regained in two hours drinking water and wine nearing
home Mozart's 40th floated to meet me and first I thought
I had a heat high then that Polly must have returned but
it was Tjitjo playing her battery radio he said I needed
a bath

get undressed   i'll heat water

poured in my "bathtub" lent by Manuel the kind of shallow enamelled bowl I remember as a child seeing my sister
bathed in England I think they are called pudding basins
after I had done all I could Tjitjo washed my back . . .

> I did need that bath although I pre-
> ferred to wash no more than once a
> week finding the accumulation of
> body-salt oil dirt less irritating than
> the feeling of sweat-stuck sand form-
> ing immediately after a bath and I did
> see the barrier of envy erected by a
> clean shirt changed every day we Tjit-
> jo and I usually shared that one basin
> each week with Damo John Ssao
> maybe a couple other men standing
> naked around it in secluded bush
> near the wells scooping up water in
> cupped hands washing each others
> backs.

November 73: walked with Tase to Twihaba to take an animal cen-
sus, sixty kay roundtrip; took no water, only one loaf of soda bread —
will rely on rainpools, and if we get no other food, milk from the cattle-
post established after rains began at Nwama. In the afternoon, temperature well over 40° C, found a pool no more than a meter in diameter, three or four centimeters deep, choked with reeds which we
bent aside to find easily 100 thumb-sized fat frogs with bright green
stripes and did not hesitate to drink half their home. Later, woke in
the night to see a silent shape move in the moonless dark to lie under
a bush twelve feet away, head resting on outstretched paws; chin on
my hands crossed at blanket edge, we studied each other until imper-
ceptibly I fell asleep and no longer saw her. In the morning I learned
the sign of female leopard.

Returning, Tase tapped each spoor with his stick, its head a heavy
burl-knob for use as a club, its end shaved sharp for digging:

> what's this one   today we'll be doing this all day   you should
> know them all by the time we get back to Kaikai

It took much longer. On our way, a hunting camp abandoned that

morning by his uncle (knowing who it was by the footprints); cracked
some of the scattered bones to eat the marrow — Tase had thrown his
club at a bird, the only meat we had seen, but missed . . .

finding in an abandoned geology camp used in   7
a premature hunt for oil on the Yukon coast in the
50s a rusted can of strawberry jam pulled open with our
fingers scooping out the contents ravenous for sugar and
fat our supply plane fog-bound for weeks at Inuvik pilot
biscuit and the caribou we shot thin in the calving season
keeping us full but unsatisfied when the plane finally arrived we ate butter by the handful and had roaring diar-
rhea all that night that never lost the light of day . . .

At Nwama, Eiffel-rust rain etched across chalcedony-green after-light
sucked out of the mid-Atlantic where the rainbow arc of the sunken
sun is gliding toward North America: I can imagine that to be an organic reality, a function of the electrical charge of light clinging to
its own perimeter and to reflections of important earth features —
Guatemalan jungles could furnish the green for those bound to that
place — wind carrying Eiffelcolor down with the shape blown into the
rain. You can't be in only one place at a time — how could you find
the way there, or ever return?

Coffee boiled for an hour in milk
constantly skimmed so that it is
like hot cocoa with a different
taste, bitter roots roasted on a fire,
and long after dark, the milking
done, huge bowls of fresh clab-
bered yogurt.

All this milk; just a month ago there was practically none; only cows
with newly dropped calves had enough so that some could be taken
for people to drink. Those were hard days:

  look at us   thinness is taking us

It was true. During the first sprinkles of the seaon — before the rain
had done anything other than raise hopes and freckle the sand — I went
hunting with Zona; we returned with only a tortoise smaller than a
fist and because it was hot and we had worked hard and I liked him
and because he had been the first to allow me to accompany him hunt-

ing and today he had said I was a real Zhu when I saw the tortoise he overlooked, I gave him a cupful of mealie meal to take 8 to his older wife who was sick and had lost her appetite; the old man so happy he strutted around saying now we will eat jerking a leg up and cutting a sharp fart with each step, everyone rolling on the ground gasping he's been eating wild onions how can he say he's hungry. It was the last time he ever hunted. Old Sana, their first children more than forty years old, grew weaker while Zona spent all nights singing and dancing over her in an attempt to drive out the illness, succeeding only in tiring himself.

The first time we hunted together, the first time I hunted here with anyone, Zona killed a steenbuck and to show I would do my share, I carried it back to camp even though the cord binding its legs cut into my shoulder. Later, lying under the shade tree by his hut, Sana smoothing ostrich-eggshell beads against her thigh with a grindstone, the younger wife, Shea, putting what appeared to be old boards to bake in hot ashes while tending a boiling pot, everybody spitting into the sand from time to time and covering it with a flick of the fingers; seeing myself in the droppings piling up under the donkey standing a few feet away because I suddenly remembered that my mother would sometimes illustrate what she meant about my being slow or lazy in learning something by telling me in German that the galloping donkey had left me behind, and thinking that the warm fertile smell that filled the air came out of those donkey droppings.

What are you putting into the ashes?

giraffe skin

Which was in fact as stiff and hard as a board hacked to pieces with an axe; and old, having been stored in the sun since it was killed not less than six months ago, but in roasting the hair burned off and the cells expanded and it became crackling just as hog skin does at home.

And in the pot?

stomach of yesterday's steenbuck

And now I became really interested because even before I learned of galloping donkeys I liked trash meat as innards were called in Texas where I grew up . . .

> my family called them that although we belonged to the class that either ate a lot of them or rationalized the absence of meat from the table by saying we don't like it all that much anyway we did have standards of course looked down on next-door neighbors who ate chicken feet fried in batter just like it was real meat after all you can go too far . . .

Oh shit! Now I've gone too far; nothing could taste so awful. This stomach wasn't cooked in its contents exactly, those were dumped out, but a thick slime of semi-liquid semi-shit clung to it when it was thrown into the pot; that smell didn't come out of the donkey. Don't complain, there's more to lose than a little piece of rubbery shit; a big chunk of credibility could go down the tube. Shove it into a cheek pocket and practice the spitting, sand-flicking technique; talk about what we will do tomorrow.

Took a walk this evening—after writing twenty-five letters today in order to send them out with the game scout who passed through unexpectedly. Lovely sunset, air washed clear by last night's rain—saw the tawny eagle again, settling for the night; in the last light, eleven kudu—females with young—came out onto the molapo,   9
played a few minutes, then ran at full tilt across to the south
side, some jumping bushes taller than themselves, vanishing up the far ridge. Had been feeling low, result of writing all those letters, measuring the distance to people and things I miss. But the walk, the eagle, the evening, the kudu brought me around.

A hundred spoor counts, dozens of hunts, days upon days lying in the shades of trees learning who is related to whom, what is going into pots; a return to the States slipped between stays at Kaikai: on the short moving stair between concourses in Grand Central I have to navigate by myself for the first time — others have conveyed me here in planes, cabs, limousines for pieces of paper, mutely exchanged for the most part — wrong currency or too few coins invariably offered, staring at greenback dollars as something foreign. Suddenly realizing that on this escalator I am confronted by more people than I have seen in nearly two years (thousands passed en route seen on the far sides of windows, mere specks in shifting landscapes); moving by rote rather than design.

In Kaikai, fewer people but missing anonymity.

*   *   *

Separate Parts

The track is never the same no matter how often I drive it. The sun shines differently every day and the wind moves sand from east to west or west to east or from some other compass point that is predictable on a seasonal basis for the subcontinent as a whole but unknowable even from minute to minute down in the dunes and thornscrub. Aardvarks, pangolins, porcupines, mice, even ants and termites constantly change the contours of the tire tracks that constitute the road; the first two destroying the constructions of the last — all moving dirt, digging for food. In the dry heat centered around September-October some of that dirt, flour fine — called dust in English but more expressively in Zhu the separated part, the same word applied to divorce — turns to mud on the eyelids, each blink serving not to clean eyeballs but to renew the thin film which forms a fifth superfluous refracting surface (the other four being the powdered insides and outsides of windshield and eyeglasses) through which one learns to navigate much as a spearfisherman does not throw at an image under water, knowing not to look at a Namaqua dove flying parallel to the window and to glance quickly at a clutch of yearling ostrich easily staying ahead at 50kph or a warthog tusker tiring after only a couple of minutes at 40. A landscape of glances, monotonous, with compelling details.

I can cover the 320 kilometers between Kaikai and Maun in under seven hours when conditions are right; usually it takes longer. Once as long as four days — three of them stuck in the mud, the rainy season state of the separated part accumulated in the crotches of dunes . . .

January 76: returning alone to Kai-kai; truck loaded with everything needed for the next five months — 400 liters of petrol, cases of wine, some food — mainly coffee plus beans and flour for bread to break the monotony of bush meals and sour milk — 100 kilos of tobacco to be distributed along with laundry and bath soap, 200 tins of bully beef for the Strasburg Supplementary Stuffing (to be fed in enormous breakfasts at my camp each morning for two weeks to a dozen volunteers, controls to insure that the results of glucose tolerance tests would not be skewed by undernourishment), the name in honor of generations of geese stuffed for their livers two tins of which are in my stock to be saved for lonesome Sundays. I had gotten through some treacherous places; more than once black muddy water had surged over the hood. The little puddle looked easy; didn't even gear down to first, two-wheel drive, riding on confidence: dead still, only a few hours left to the day, no use to try digging out now — time to celebrate the arrival of Nancy's Christmas package which I had received in Maun, her fruit cake — along with a bottle of sherry dug out of the supplies. During the night, thunderstorms, half a foot of water added to the

mud, in the morning only the tops
of tires seen above the slush . . .

*   *   *

Rain

Seemingly endless days of dripping rains are both welcome and dreary
here, just as everywhere. In some years — perhaps two out of five or
six, sometimes none at all for five or six years in a row, sometimes
two or three back-to-back — February can be like that; by mid-March
people are weary of the constant damp. Termites claim the poles and
thatch of huts built on too-shallow dunes, where compacted sands
of melapo are strong enough to support underground tunnel structures; a gritty residue sifts down — wood dust from their chewing, sand
from tubular passageways cemented with termite spit constructed to
shield their makers from the sun as they work their ways up walls
to the roof. Such a hut needs to be beaten: its contents taken out and
its roof and walls flayed — as we used to beat carpets hung over back-
yard clotheslines. Boxes, anything gnawable, must be balanced on
small rocks or on old oil filters saved for such a use when replaced,
gotten off the ground. It's best to abandon such a hut and build a
new one.

Clothes and bedding stay wet, reinforced by sweat that can't evaporate
in the muggy heat; mildew invades leather; sinew bowstrings become
soft and slack; arrow and spear bindings unravel; seldom-used wooden
utensils grow green mould and must be discarded. Drowned flies float
in cups of coffee.

Here there is no Groundhog's Day on which to say maybe in six weeks
the sun will break through and daffodils bloom. But other things are
said that mean the same:

> now shortly   in a month perhaps   when moon returns to this
> phase to this position up there   now shortly it will be
> Tobe when nuts and fruits will be ripe and garden mel-   10
> ons   sun will go along its north path   will not be so
> hot   there will be days days days days days without rain   we
> will take horses to hunt eland and giraffe   it will be fat times
> we will pick a few ears of green corn just to taste them   will leave
> most standing on the stalks until the cold of Guum begins when

you can chew on the boiled hard kernels of a single mealie-cob from mid-morning til noon

Before the end of April, the wet season begins to blow away; you can watch it go. Clouds form in the afternoon heat at the tops of thermal columns — evaported from the moisture in the sand — to be carried westward by upper winds, removing water from the land. As the sun sinks, its heat is deflected, evaporation stops, and at twilight the sky is clear again; by mid-May, when Guum begins, there is no dew . . .

> In 73, rains began early — at the end of the second week of October — after three years of severe heat and drought. I had thought the vegetation would never recover and didn't believe Manuel's description of Kaikai in the rain. The wells went dry on seven days that September. Returning from his snares, on the day I caught the tortoise, Zona took a different direction — straight to a rainpool called Kkao zzi, hyaena shit; while we walked, he shoved a stick into the body of the tortoise — between carapace and plastron, the upper and lower shells, where the tail and hind legs come out — and now he stuck the other end of the stick into the sand beside the pool (the animal's legs continuing to walk uselessly in the air — hours later it was still alive when put to roast in ashes); without a word, Zona stripped naked and walked into the knee-deep, opaque water — I was just seconds behind — and silently, with only an occasional grunt of satisfaction, or a murmured this is good, we scrubbed our skins and hair with handfuls of sand scooped from the muddy bottom . . .

The atmosphere [at the cattleposts] must be something like the better folkloric elements of the Old West. People dress more casually, are not so concerned about modesty; women tease their men about exaggerated contortions while in trance; men play a highly animated version of scissor-paper-stone, saying of the loser that he has become a woman. There is constant movement between cattleposts and Kaikai; everyone riding donkeys — mothers and fathers with a child or two in front on the donkey's shoulders, between the reins; sometimes another, older, child behind the saddle.

I don't ride donkeys. Donkeys and I don't understand each other. I ride horses . . .

Some of my friends have had opportunities to make comparisons —
with the Old West; when in Maun, we often go to films shown at
one of the safari camps; many are westerns. Kamko's first was *Butch
Cassidy and the Sundance Kid*; Damo Saao and John were there.
Translating, I kept up a continuous jabber

That man, he loves the girl and. . . . now those two are trying to
get away from those guys who are following their spoor. . . .

shutup   we can see what's going on

. . . .

see Kamko he's looking closely   seeing things   tomorrow he'll paint
about this

He did; painted the most lyrical moment of the film: the bicycle scene,
handstand, backwards on the handlebars; but Kamko, unlike Damo
understands not a single word of English.

Snakes are the protectors of rain; the penalty for disrespect can be
severe: Nisa's death was divined to have been retribution for the killing and eating of the python at Ggo. In the hot, rainy months snakes
give live birth and are seen often . . .

Throughout Southern Africa, they have been associated with rain, py-
thons and mambas; it seems may have been so far into the past: snakes
with horned heads and human limbs are painted on cave walls at
Giant's Castle high on the Drakensberg (try to find out where the name
came from "Dragon Mountain," is it European mythology transferred
to the southern end of Africa, or did the Boers hear stories from people
already there); they are painted too on the bare rocks of the high Brand-
berg from whose flanks the Atlantic, 120 km to the west, can be seen
in the day and at night lights of ships passing Cape Cross which Por-
tugal claimed in 1484. Some of these paintings may be a thousand
years old or more, and all are hundreds of kilometers away from where
any Zhu has ever been; yet, one day — before I had seen these old
paintings on the rocks — Kamko painted snake-persons for me.

At Tsodilo, deep holes extend far back into the rock, some hold permanent pools of rain water: Samanchai said the big mamba that lived
there guarded the pool against those to whom god refused the water,
but the snake wouldn't hurt anyone who respected it. He had once

found a leopard dead in the pool, killed by the mamba. Ssao John Kamko Damo agreed such things were true; while a ten-foot mamba, thick as my arm, slid slowly toward us, no more than two meters away, and curled under a rock.

Only much later — telling about it in a city, the foreign atmosphere adding an absent danger — did I think of the fear that was supposed to be there.

Reading the Ground

Following an animal's spoor you enter unobtrusively into its private life for a moment; accumulate such moments, many repetitions, many conditions, piece together individual behaviors; learn a species. Seeing where this cheetah stopped to scratch, where it inspected an empty hole in the side of a termite hill (remember the tenants of other holes, what the cheetah was looking for), where it lay down under a terminalia bush — entering its space for a short time; the animal's image as real a presence as if its body were here . . .

we once followed a pair of jackal spoor to the point where they killed a steenbuck Ninnow told me that long ago he had seen where a lone jackal had killed a kudu fawn so he knew that was possible but seldom happened at Dobe in September 79 Maswe and I saw where a lion cub had killed a hare dragged it under an acacia disemboweled it and buried the entrails before eating . . .

a common habit of lions which Zhu know routinely from reading the ground. They aren't the only people who know such things, Herero can read spoor as well as any Zhu . . .

Tjitjo's saddled donkey slipped away one moonless night talking we didn't hear it go with a flashlight he followed its spoor through those of dozens of other donkeys goats cattle and brought it back . . .

Sometimes Alone

I'm not always sure whether it's the pale light seeping into the sky or the cackling of francolin cocks — louder, harsher than more distant roosters — that first wakes me when I'm alone in my camp — then doves, hornbills; all the avian racket of desert dawns (there'll be dispute about this — not all deserts have so many birds, not all parts of this desert. Not everyone remembers the same things): rolling out of blankets, knocking shoes together to shake out scorpions (only one in how-many-hundred mornings?); fire going before the sun appears. I like to be well into a cup of coffee before Ssao John Damo arrive, the kettle continuing to boil for them, each hunkering down with a cup in turn; on leisurely mornings when nothing is planned we may drink three maybe four cups each, half-liter cups, while we talk, later catch up with neglected housekeeping while we decide how to spend the day.

Different waking in their camps: same background sounds, but legs entwined with others ringing the fire, blankets laid across shoulders, even in summer, waiting for the sun and water to boil.

Different in bush camps: usually no coffee although I'm expected to bring enough for the first day or two. Same sounds, same fire, same blankets waiting for the sun; repeating, probably for the thousandth time, certainly ten times this morning, the trivia that reminds the group it belongs together . . .

> December 79 at Twihaba beginning to move in the morning Tase calls to the others

>> see you all   see that bush there   that's where we Twi and I saw the female leopard spoor   it lay down in the night under this branch just here and looked at us   then it went off along this way   Twi saw it in the night but I was asleep

>> Aie, see me! Do you know why he was asleep and I wasn't?

>> sure truly   i'll tell them   i took his second blanket so he had only one and was cold

*   *   *

Yesterday evening, standing with Ssao on the slightly elevated flank of the dune south of the wells:

Kaikai is beautiful now that the rains have come.

yes truly Kaikai is a beautiful place put a store there a bank there a clinic over by the school

That is not what I saw. I saw colors, forms, light — only incidentally trees, leaves and grass, sand, clouds; certainly I saw no buildings.

But now, watching Tishe, I see that Ssao saw more clearly. It's all very well to dignify rags; they remain rags. Everyone sees that. Kao sees that and prefers whole cloth.

*   *   *

Toma's Job

A high fence separates Botswana from Namibia: seventeen strands of barbed and smooth wire stretched taut across desert miles, hundreds of miles long; built in 1969 to replace an older, ordinary, four-strand fence. There's no doubt the fence helps control the spread of foot-and-mouth disease among cattle — elephants occasionally break down a short section; small diggers tunnel under and other animals — warthogs, for instance — use the passage; steenbuck and duiker dive between strands. There are turnstiles at the points where ancient footpaths — old wagon roads intersect the fenceline but these are seldom used, people finding it easier to follow duiker through the strands. But cattle seldom get through.

There's also no doubt the fence helps control movement between people . . .

*   *   *

what is the biggest place you have seen

I'm not sure. New York, or London maybe, perhaps Tokyo in a country called Japan. You have seen Johannesburg and Durban, know how many people stay there. Each of those places I named — New York, London, Tokyo — has more people than are between here and Johannesburg and all the way to Durban.

we knew there must be big places   we had to carry so
many bodies

Yet, 300 years ago, New York wasn't unlike Kaikai; cowpaths marked
the routes that people took to wells and cornfields — later swoll into
streets without intention; retaining names   like Water and Milk.

> Still; it was a surprise, in these
> southern tropics near Capricorn,
> to see the Big Dipper rise upside
> down just above the northern ho-
> rizon at ten in a March night.

Often for weeks at a time I left my camp to live "just like them" as
far as satisfying external daily needs are concerned — sharing the same
pot, doing without when there was nothing in the pot, getting what
I needed — from string to sticks for toilet paper — from the bush. It
is not a difficult life; there were times when its virtues cast the defects
of contemporary America into sharp negative focus — at those times
my sweat would stink with apprehension, not wanting to think of the
adjustments I would have to make . . .

> when I came to Kowri with the storm and dusk look-
> ing for help to dig me out of the mud I was invited
> to stay the night in the hut of an old couple Kusaa
> and Dikao we sat cross-legged beside a smokeless
> fire over which tea brewed quietly exchanging gossip
> taking the evening meal of clabbered milk they took
> spare sheets with a delicate floral print from a trunk
> made a bed for me on a cowhide mat their unintru-
> sive attentiveness that of gracious hosts anywhere
> a Chinese ink painting in motion spare economical
> brush strokes essential structure in place filled in by
> participants . . .

But I did not always enjoy living like them. Often I would yearn for
a French goat cheese and crusty bread, espresso in a Cafe Paradiso,
a gallery, any film. My friends were aware of those times: haunched
around a fire, my mind would sometimes stray from a conversation,

someone would say

he doesn't hear now   he is in his own place

They found that reasonable.

Notes

1. On the second day after my first arrival in Kaikai, Manuel Nguvauva, who had been away visiting in Mahopa, returned. He had completed sixth grade at Maun Secondary School and knew some English. He became my interpreter. It was his presence that allowed me to understand what was happening there.

2. Zhu is an unwritten language without an agreed upon orthography. For this reason, and to distinguish speakers in passages of dialogue, I have adopted the convention of using only lower case letters (except for names) and no punctuation for Zhu speech. I have extended that convention to Herero speech, although Herero has been written — in an orthography devised by missionaries — for 100 years. I have also greatly simplified the spelling of Zhu and Herero names.

3. Tow is Zhu for motor vehicle, from mahowtow which is Herero taken from auto, with the noun prefix ma added.

4. The other two were Polly Wiessner, then a graduate student in anthropology at the University of Michigan, who studied gift-giving networks, and Dwight Reed, a mathematician-anthropologist at UCLA interested in kinship.

5. Zhu children are incorporated into their social group by being given the name of one member of a specified set of same-sex relatives. A firstborn son usually receives the name of his paternal grandfather, a firstborn daughter that of her paternal grandmother; secondborn children receive the names of maternal grandparents. Thereafter, parents' older siblings take precedence. The name-giver is called Big-Name of the name receiver who is the Little-Name of that person. In English, these terms are usually glossed grandfather/grandmother and grandchild respectively. Zhu have a system of kinship extension called universalizing by anthropologists; that is, all persons with whom they have frequent contact, including anthropologists, are given a place in a Zhu kin network through the mechanism of being given a name. Such persons acquire, thereby, a namegiver-grandparent along with the kinship coterie of the name giver.

6. Archival sources are comparatively meager for Ngamiland and are almost silent regarding social and indigenous economic organization, although those that do exist contain much information regarding Euro-

pean trade. I needed to know as much as possible about the colonial and precolonial history of the region and therefore incorporated extensive archaeological survey and excavation into my research program.

7. The Arctic is littered with abandoned remains of searches for minerals. In July 1961, I was a member of a four-man party excavating a site at the mouth of the Firth River in Yukon Territory. On one of our exploring trips, we found one of these and ransacked it for anything useful.

8. Mealie meal is corn meal that is ground fine and cooked as porridge; it is also called mouli.

9. Molapo is a Setswana word meaning dry water course.

10. Tobe is the end of the rain season corresponding to autumn, generally mid-March to mid-May. This is the season of ripening for most of the principle wild foods as well as for domestic crops. Large animals are most easily hunted at this time and cows produce much milk. It is the rich season. Guum is winter, more like Indian Summer; June-August.

Victor Flach

DISPLACINGS & WAYFARINGS:
Metaphorisms & Tetratypes

"Here am I am here." The journey of not moving, the speed of
Place: or Placement. But it's not the transience that's remembered. It's the Place of Events that constitute History rather than
the Events themselves—which are transient. The journey of
Geography. History as a matter of Place. Nothing can be *Held
in Place* for very long, but Everything is Held *BY* Place: Events
are held by Place—as on a canvas or page. This is the Motion
of Direction, rather than the motion of Moving. Paul Klee says
"The father of the Arrow is the question: How can I extend my
range in that direction?".... Plot is never the whole shape, the
lump of structure, the total figuration taken altogether at-once.
But the Seasons must be *traversed*, moved through: even when
the Seasons are inside ourselves the passage occurs. But *whose*
passage—inside or outside ourselves. The journey is Reciprocal.... When we move through Space, we say "Time Passes,"
but when we are With-Time, we say "Small World." The more
I *Grow*, the smaller the World, and the more we *Die*, the more
time passes. Time-passing is really the *Worlds* which are past,
and the smallest World is my enormous unmoving *Present*.
[Growing is the realization of Patterns as Principle. So] which
aspect of the Seasons is most significant: their *Passage* from one
Season to the next, or the absolute *Recurrence of their Pattern*—
the Coming and Going of their Gradual Passage, or the Being
of their Patterned Recurrence?.. Both-at-Once...

VF, from "A Lofty Discourse" (May 1958), *IN/SERT 4* (1962)

I. TOWARD CULTURE OF PLACES*

"To start with the local for analogy, and arrive at the universal *locale*, place, placement, ordering of one's own experience through form — that may be called truly Human."   Anna Lex (VI,28,iii)

"It is this consciousness of destruction that gives so peculiar a character and such a touching beauty to the solitude of America.... Thoughts of the savage, natural grandeur that is going to come to an end, become mingled with splendid anticipations of the triumphant march of civilization."
Alexis de Tocqueville (1831)

"I charge you to spare, preserve and cherish some portion of your primitive forests; for when these are cut away I apprehend they will not easily be replaced."   Horace Greeley (1851)

"I enter a swamp as a sacred place.... A town is saved, not more by the righteous men in it than by the woods and swamps that surround it."
Henry David Thoreau (1861)

"Thousands of tired, nerve-shaken, over-civilized people are beginning to find out that going to the mountains is going home..." John Muir (1898)

Might poetic analogies between Earth Places and Seasons start practical awareness toward an Ecocompass and Geocalendar: how shall Earth weather the changes brought by severe forestcutting and over-grazing — where geographic climates of rainvalley erosion and desert-drought become overextended in both *duration and areas* (such as Brazil and Africa)? What if archetypal GEOSEASONS occur in all combinations and interfacings — with extreme latitude for thermal variables, and for north temperate vista bias? [Cf. "Archetypal Principles" quadrant in "Habitative Typology" section following.]

(1) Like dawn from the east, *Spring's* bright sources sprout and pour from *Mountain/meadow/valleys*;

(2) absorbed, as in a "southern" day, by *Summer* heat and hiatus laying in the open dry *Desert/prairie/plains* (and *tundra* or *ice-plains* at very different temperatures);

(3) metabolized, as dusk rolls west over ocean horizon, like *Fall's* flux and processes rise and fall longest and strongest at *Sea/lake/rivers*; and

(4) "north's" *Winter* darkness is shared by enclosures of the organic architecture of rich woody and fruitful *Rainforest or Jungles* (even when tropical).

---

*This section, originally entitled "Metaphorisms Toward a Culture of Place" — along with Richard Fleck's "Psychic Lands and Mythic Falls" — first appeared in *Wyoming Quarterly*, Vol.I, No.2, Summer 1975, edited by Catherine Mealey.

Range is range and Fertile Valley and Mountain Plain have different eco-systems, different functions. But in the reciprocity of Human Individuality with Natural Environment, what of *concentrated* grazing and tilling? Fertile Farm as *fixed* Place, Ranging Ranch as Place to *range*: Spirit-of-Place.

What if "Farm" means the Man cultivating the Land: and "Ranch" means the Land cultivating the Man? Then does Farmer imbue (despoil?) the Land in spirit of his own image, for his needs: and is Rancher imbued by the spirit of the Land's image, wrangling his needs as he can with minimum modification of Land's Nature? "Expressionist" Farmer impressing himself on the world, and "Impressionist" Rancher impressed by the world?

Or the reverse? Farmer *cultivating* Land—caring for it, investing in it, putting something back for what he's displaced—*all Universe operating as continual displacings*! Land cultivating Rancher—caring for him, as he takes from the Land with less return of substance to it, relying on Nature to replenish itself as it can. Farmer shaping the Land in cooperation with Nature: Rancher shaped by the Land—low-population Technoman displacing the low-population Aborigine and Mythic Land's bounty of wild game with gun, fort-house, railroad, barbwire for his cattle and sheep in the taking? Or for the protein and wool?

Or for uranium and oil? Then continuing the process, is it inevitable the Rancher in his turn be displaced *in certain areas* by the Energy and Mineral Strippers? Even the old Timber Barons have slowly become Farmers with their Reforestation.

As Stewardship gradually displaces Ownership (since latter is ultimately impossible)—at least two viable relations of Man-to-Place seem to emerge? (a) The Aboriginal or Rural *Spirit Land*—referring to magic or reverential influence of Land on Man's consciousness, spirit, as a cooperative rapport of low-density groups with their environs—suggests contrasts to the adverse influences of (b) Uncultivated Place-Exploitation (rooted in fear and greed?), and (c) Unmodulated High-density Turbulent Place (as some urban centers?): and another viable option of (d) a Cultivated Technology permitting an appropriately Modulated Optimum-density *Reciprocal Place*. [Cf. "Anthrotopia" section following.]

Technology, as development and use of Tools—extension of Man himself—must not be seen as bug-a-boo, or barrier to attainment of Reciprocal Place: but rather Man's *means* of arrival. After awkwardly obtrusive (industrial) growing-pains, a Cultivated Technology whose tendency to (1) *Completed Chemistries & Physics* (whole-cycling as "recycling" and "by-products" rather than "pollution" and "waste"), (2) *Miniaturization*, (3) *Closer and Accelerated Connections between all Elements and Phases of Cycling* (inner-, intra-, inter-system efficiencies and distributions), and (4) *Custom Mass-Production by Computer-Jigging* (individual wants filled by robotics) bodes prospects for the increasingly invisible, unobtrusive character of the invisible, intangible *relations* and *functions* themselves — increasingly analogous to Nature ("' Form follows function' — but if the functions are invisible, then the forms will become invisible" — R. Buckminster Fuller). Then the new sense of *Mythic Place* must include the new technologies as integral with priorities in Individual-and-Universe relationships. Clarification of proper Land-use and Distribution Functions may permit Individual Consciousness to re-engage the eternally *Inherent Where* — the Magic of Roots, Locus, Situs, Position: from which and in which matrix one may *take his Position*. A Cultural Force-Field of Crossroads or Juncture, and of Environ or Surround — decreasingly apparent to casual passers-through, since the deeply indigenous remains more hidden: All Earth and Outward Journeying as ultimate *Mythoscape*, foundations of the Time Culture.

As free-flowing access to clear orderly Universal Principle becomes more universally important in World Culture (Culture of Persistent Now) — as by selective technologic freeing-up and accommodation of "Third World" developing countries and the consequent natural Distribution (dissemination, dissipation) of artificial Power (political and military) — is there a tendency for non-feudal, genuinely *Indigenous Cultures* to flourish and emerge? Does Individual and Cultural *uniqueness and difference* seem (paradoxically) permitted, sustained, carried, and encouraged by more *selectively standard and universal* technologic means (tools, like home-based information-processors, computers, network-terminals, etc) — *IF*, and only if, that carefully appropriate *selectivity* is not itself Exploitative and Bureaucratic?

VF. (14-20.IV.75)

"Land and sea are the warp and woof of the world."
"Gardens should be a series of *diverse* secrecies."
Table Talk of Ian Hamilton Finlay (1985)

"Let us stay/...where the unfit/ Contrarious moods of men.../...permit/
A place to stand and love in for a day/"
　　　Elizabeth Barrett Browning, *Sonnets From the Portuguese* (1850)

- "ANY who live stand alone in one place together."
- "Are you there?"　/　"Yes, but not here."
- "Why you running, pal? You'll be all tuckered out by the time you get
  where you're goin'."
  "Where I'm goin'? Do you reckon I'd be blurrin' ground like this if I had
  me any place to go."　　　　　Kenneth Patchen, *Wonderings* (1971)

"Humans live best when each has his place to stand, when each knows where
he belongs in the scheme of things and what he may achieve. Destroy the
place and you destroy the person."
　　　Bene Gesserit Teaching — Frank Herbert, *Heretics of Dune (V)* (1984)

II. ANTHROTOPIA　:　PATTERNS OF HUMAN HABITAT
Constellations of Human Places of Emergence, Divergence, Convergence, Commerce — Shifting Dominance at Various Stages of Civilization (Societal Phases)

*HABITYPES**
Behavioral Habitats
as "Neighborhoods"

*FOUR DOMINANT OVERLAPPING
NETWORKS OF HUMAN PLACES*
Topotypal Networks of Anthrogeographic Centers :
Anthropolitan Congregations and Emanations

Habitatal Habitats

(1) *SITE-RESOURCE CENTERS : Geopolitan Nodes*

　　　Aboriginal Centers of Sacred or Unique Natural
　　　Phenomena/Modern Resources-Preserves-Resorts—
　　　　eg, arise as Geographic Conditions:
　　　land/crops (timber, etc)/parks; mountains/mines/
　　　ski-retreats; rivers/hydroelectrics/boating-resorts;
　　　island, oasis warm-climates/beach, desert retire-
　　　ment-communities; etc...

Habitantial Habitats

(2) *MANUFACTURE-CONSUMER CENTERS :*
　　　Metropolitan Nodes (Metro = Mother Cities)
　　　Urban Centers of Manufacture/Maintenance/
　　　Local Distribution/Consumption —
　　　　eg, arise as Inner-Terminae (of industry) along
　　　transport routes of rivers, roads, railroads, high-
　　　ways, with much local commerce; etc...

---

　*Cf. *(A) Neighborhoods*, the factored Habitats in "Contextualism & the Habitative Typology" section following.

Habitative Habitats (3) *EXCHANGE-ARCHIVE CENTERS :*
Cosmopolitan Nodes (No inventive ideas but
those in exchange & fashion)
World Centers of Commerce/Government (usually)/
Communications Media/Cultural Repositories —
eg, arise as International Ports (of exchange)
usually near major coasts where shipping & bank-
ing, fashion-setting & wholesaling, government
seats & embassies, publishing & broadcasting,
libraries & museums flourish; ports along cara-
van- sea- air- & space-lanes; etc...

Habitudinal Habitats (4) *INDIGENOUS-INVENTIVE CENTERS :*
Egopolitan Nodes

Often Rural & Suburban Centers defined as "centers" only by the Independent Individuals and
Ideas that arise from each specific locale —
but eg, whatever matrix of "neighborhood"
spawns & nourishes wonder, experience, ideas, &
deeds of inventive imaginations or individual
achievers; Jefferson's Monticello, Dickinson's Amherst, Edison's Menlo Park, the Wrights' Kitty-
hawk, etc...

(Research & Learning Centers mostly arise at 2
and 3, with Specialties at 1 and 4...)
VF. (17.V.85)

"The landscape of a people is the greatest factor in molding their habits,
their looks, their physical and spiritual attributes."
Edward Weston (1955)

"We are the children of our landscape. It dictates behavior and even thought
in the measure to which we are responsive to it."
Lawrence Durrell, *Alexandria Quartet* (1959)

"Every living thing must have its HABITATION...domiciles in which to
shelter themselves from [weathers], to which to flee from danger, and in
which to rear their young...and store...winter supplies....Even every
seed...has its own chamber and bed in its paternal homestead...till it can
go forth [to] a permanent...place. The very hills have their eternal resi-
dences, and waters their ever-occupied abiding-places, while earth, and every
sister planet, and celestial sphere, each traverses its own pathway...Thus,
[all] thing[s] have their own homes, and in turn become abodes....This great
home law[:] Endowed with the primitive faculty called "inhabitiveness"...
COMPELLING [man] to provide some abiding-place, which [he] MUST
HAVE...as much as breath or sleep....as much as...food or clothes —
[which are] only cloth houses.

"HABITATIONS CORRESPOND WITH...CHARACTERISTICS [OF THEIR INHABITANTS] perfectly...so that the latter can...be predicated from the former....Of course this general rule has many modifications and exceptions [for man] from necessity, habit, aversion to change the abode of earlier years, or even sheer inattention.

"Man [is] also...endowed with a building faculty [and] nature...render[s] the act of] building itself most pleasurable....This pleasure is consequent on gratifying those two primitive faculties, Inhabitiveness and Constructiveness, along with several others; without the former of which he would never wish to build if he could; and without the latter, could not if he would. How perfect this...arrangement..! Then let it be cultivated by all."

Orson Squire Fowler (1809-87), *A Home For All...*
(1847 & 1853, Fishkill, N.Y.)

III. CONTEXTUALISM & THE HABITATIVE TYPOLOGY*

"Every sacred space implies a hierophany, an interruption of the sacred that results in detaching a territory from the surrounding cosmic milieu and making it qualitatively different. (p26)

"It must be understood that cosmicization of unknown territories is always a consecration; to organize a space is to repeat the paradigmatic work of the gods. (p32)

"Establishment in a particular place, organizing it, inhabiting, are acts that presuppose a...choice — the choice of the universe that one is prepared to assume by 'creating' it. Now, this universe is always the replica of the paradigmatic universe created and inhabited by the gods; hence it shares in the sanctity of the god's work. (p34)

"To settle in a territory, to build a dwelling, demands a vital decision.... For what is involved is undertaking the creation of the world that one has chosen to inhabit. Hence it is necessary to imitate the work of the gods, the cosmogony. (p51)

"In all traditional cultures, the habitation possesses a sacred aspect by the simple fact that it reflects the world....In other words, cosmic symbolism is found in the very structure of the habitation. (p53)

"If a 'construction' is to endure (be it house, temple, tool, etc.), it must be animated, it must receive life and a soul. (p56)

"There is, then, a sacred space, and hence a strong, significant space; there are other spaces that are not sacred and so are without structure or con-

---

*These notes — developed during lectures and consultation with James Mai, who began vividly employing the ideas in the visual works of his Exhibition and accompanying Catalog for his Master of Fine Arts Thesis at the University of Wyoming Department of Art — are dedicated to him in appreciation of his dedication to the potentialities of the Habitative System.

sistency, amorphous....For it is the break effected in space that allows the world to be constituted, because it reveals the fixed point, the central axis for all future orientation." (pp20-21)

Mircea Eliade, *The Sacred and the Profane* (1957)

Sacred Places are natural and-or constructed MICROCOSMS set-apart by the animating Mind from their surroundings by some con-textualizing boundary. Usually Habitats or Nodes for Ritual behavior, they consist of some combination of four basic conditions with some dominance thereof:

(1) the *Omphalos*, or axial Center of the World from and around which emanates and turns its influential aura and order, often symbolicly marking some great *event* as does the Bodhi-tree or Lotus columns (to be distinguished from Generative phallic or lingam associations of most menhirs or obelisks);

(2) the circumferentially bounding *Wall* itself, differentiating its sacred withinness from the immediate withoutness, like even an encompassing line scribing a rudimentary *temple* or a natural or manmade circle of stones — thus *circle→kirk→church* (to be distinguished from Receptive mandorla or yoni associations of most Earth Mother caves or graves, womb-tomb formations);

(3) the axial, circumambient or labyrinthine *Pathways* within or throughout the enclosure for devotional, often processional, *pil-grimage* rituals, to one or a series of "stations" (to be distin-guished from the other Processive "Mythic Sojourns" such as the testing pursuit of the *quest*, discovery explorations of *odyssey*, and visionary inventive enterprise of the *sally* — see "Toward Culture of Sojourns" section following);

(4) the sacred *Gate* or entrance-way into the sanctum, usually ori-ented to one of the four cardinal directions and connected to *ini-tiation passage* from the mundane, earthly, to the holy, heavenly (to be distinguished from Formative associations of ex-pressive apertures opening outward, doorways and windows facing out — or the speaking mouth as squared ex-pressor in the Chinese ideo-gram, etc. Cf. G.R. Levy, *The Gate of Horn*, 1948).

Temples, as microcosms housing their symbolic Personifications of the forces of the macrocosm, function by the paradigm *"as within, so without"* — which is not quite so deceptively reversible as the Medieval version "as above, so below," and v.v.; and within which *tholoi*, the microcosmic rituals of communion ask and thank the forces for sacred — or profane — needs and hopes through their mediating Per-sonae. But may we inhabit even more inclusive and interconnected habitats?

All our Habitation in Territorial Worlds mediating all surrounding and interpenetrating Macro-cosmic and Micro-cosmic interactions requires a sense that all structural relation-ships operate only as *Re-contextualizations*. Since every part is itself a whole and every whole falls apart as only part of some larger whole, Part-Wholes are the leaky portholes that sink existential-ships. But CONTEXTS function as *Contextual Completions*—analogies for a "Totality" that can never be known—and their *Constituent Contexts*—particularities—of which they are composed. For the Composer in any media-form, structural contexts have significance for how generalizing from finding contextual patterns-in-particular-complexity seems more fruitful than reductive abstraction from and with "parts" (with reference to resultant craft-works as "Pieces")—and how concrete particularities are the result of prior structural combinations which compoundingly permit still other contexts, and, in their referential analogousness, how they model and engender unanticipated recombinations outside and beyond themselves to ever more inclusive contexts. Except for "Dipper" constellations pouring galactic "Milky Way" of "Starry Snowflakes" of feathery hexagonal watercrystals or "Tadpole" spermatozoa, etc—*nearly all micro- and macro-levels smaller or larger than the very narrow zone of directly experiential human-scale events remain quite ABSTRACTLY GENERALIZED as structural relationships*—with only scientific nomenclatures and numeric designations, but metaphorically unspecific or unnamed as descriptively thingful object-identities: especially abstract to the configuratively symbolizing left-hemisphere brain, full of eider-down feathers picturing specific webfooted waterfowl or grandparents' pillows and quilts—rather than the figuratively structural-relational patterning right-brain's quasar-to-quark *Geometries*, which are precisely what *compound* to compose feathers and starguided duck migrations and reproduction in the first place.

Nature tends to operate by overlapping and shifting *Contextual Thresholds-of-Influence* of extremely efficient-complexity—the increasingly accurate and comprehensive experience of which, Individual Mind tries to model by its analogous tendency to operate by sliding expandable/contractable, dimensionally portable/re-shapable *Contextual Frames-of-Reference*—which, as structures of comparable efficient-complexity are developed, may model experiences not yet experienced! Contextual *Referencing* is the root of all metaphoric meaning and invention: e.g., "beginnings-and-endings"—themselves the primal metaphors for contextual completions—may act as framing discontinuities, the contextual discreteness of which permits further interactive referencing *between* others and beyond themselves in ways that a continuous melding of fused content-areas toward an homogenous unity never can. But Contexts—like environing habitats—are not described nor circumscribed by hard and simple boundaries around any isolated or static "things," which would lead to stereotypic labeling and pigeonholing for doctrinaire truths.

Contextualizing refers to the *dynamic* (framing) of certain *fields-of-activity* (processes) functioning with sufficient difference from surrounding fields of activity, such that, although the fields and actions themselves may not ultimately be discrete(?), the interactive (referential) *relations* between them may *function* discretely—including *constituent* contexts, and even conditions of apparently non-discrete continuous-gradient nature. This involves Grouping/Regrouping and Figure/Field Structures, including those discrete enough to seem like "things," which are actually *conceptual nodes* in relational contexts. And con-cepts can only be constructed and held by crossreferencing some dominant combination of per-ceptual modes (Visual, Tactile, Kinesthetic, Verbal)—the first metaphoric referent of which is the identifying designation and handle involved in *naming*. The mind seems to have a natural propensity for naming things, places, processes, etc—which emphatically is not limited to *verbal* naming: one has only to think of the "adjectival" degrees of specificity of some pictorial identity, or the musical configuration of some tune. Although we give names to actions and relationships, the nominative function might be thought of as referring to the subject and object *terms* of the contextualizing sentence: in this way, "things" are the nouns which the verbs predicate in relational contexts. (Cf. VF's *Contextualist Manifesto*, 1982)

"The...eye.../ Doth glance from...earth to heaven,/ And, as imagination bodies forth/ The form of things unknown, the poet's pen/ Turns them to shapes, and gives to airy nothing/ A local habitation and a name."
Wm Shakespeare, *Midsummer Night's Dream*, V.1.

"Contextualizing seems abstract until you think about what, where, how and why you live: the habitative metaphor lets you directly feel the world's contextual structures working within and around yourself."

So in Spring 1983, the earlier notion of contextuality gets much more *concretely* contextualized as a HABITATIVE SYSTEM, by cross-referencing and compounding my previous typologic and systemic explorations of Archetypal Processes and Forms with Structural Referencing:

A. ARCHETYPAL PRINCIPLES

I. Generative Principle	II. Principle of Agency (Receptor/Actor Principle)
III. Processive Principle	IV. Formative Principle

B. WORLDS OF MEANING

1. Natural (Prior Source)	2. Individual (Direct Experience)
3. Societal (Zeitgeist)	4. Cultural (Weltanschauung)

C. MODES OF MEANING

1. Information (Data)	2. Belief (Not Given Faiths)
3. Knowledge (Cognition)	4. Wisdom (Vision built on the Patterns)

D. HABITATIVE SYSTEM

1. HABITAT	2. HABITANT
–Environ –Group –Phenomena	–Occupant –Member –Composer
3. HABITATION	4. HABITUDE
–Occupancy –Participating –Theory	–Occupation –Performance –Practice

The Habitative System presents the minimum necessary conditions for any complete contextualizing complex: since every individual inevitably participates in multiple habitations, it offers a *concrete experiential set* of relationships which can be structured in various particular media-forms to model the image-idea of Habitation as *univer-sal principle.*

(1) HABITAT — Each largest encompassing context of dominant concern which "defines" the parameters and properties of that behavior-complex belonging to it — contained by it; a relatively complete self-regulating environment which in varying degrees shapes the form and habitational behavior of constituent habitants...

(2) HABITANT — That which behaves, interactively integral with habitat and other inhabitants; component or constituent of habitat HAVING particular capabilities which selectively correspond to, and in varying degrees shape and other-wise change potentials of, its habitats...

(3) HABITATION — Behavior itself, in general; the mutually interactive com-plex of event-exchanges between habitant and habitat, and between habitant and other inhabitants; occupancy...

(4) HABITUDE — Patterns of behavior; the unique shapes or forms *con-sequent from* the forces or patterns of mutually inter-active habitation between habitant and habitat, and *necessary to* synergetic and regenerative strategies; ac-crued forms of habit — e.g., perhaps completed *works* as forms of their author's habits of mind, which now on their own in the world, may find their habitudinal purpose as new contributive habitat...

As relational ideas or principles are given more concrete image-identity or terminology — such as particularizing the contextualist no-tion to the habitative system — the roles of the operative images or terms become more fixed in their operative or functional interrela-tionships and referencing: that is, since *the multiplicity of inter- and counter-relationships at work in any form-complex are limited in direct proportion to the configurative particularity of the entities involved,* it is easy to see how a habitant may inhabit a habitat by definition, but initially it may be more difficult to imagine how the imaginative mind inhabiting a habitant may itself be a *habitat* of image-ideas. Therefore, what seems to be happening is that the *types* constituting the habitative system (habitat, habitant, habitation, habitude) are simultaneously interacting by means of an exactly analogous system of habitative *modes.* In other words, the *conditions* suggested by these terms are at every instant interacting or interchanging as and with their analogous *role-functions*: the terms must be seen and employed as both states or conditions *and* as a shifting compound overlay of roles or modes of interaction. Perhaps a rudimentary list of FAC-TORED HABITATIVE OPERATIONS with tentative descriptive clues may be suggestive:

(A) *"Neighborhoods"*

Habitatal Habitat — the inherently unique qualities of the place make the habitat what it is; habitat's inherent spirit *is* the habitat...

Habitantial Habitat — habitant *is* habitat — as for ideas or diseases...

Habitative Habitat — inhabited habitat — as the traffic makes the city...

Habitudal Habitat — form of the habitude, or "ritual" *is* habitat — as the magic contained in the rite, or worship contained in the liturgy...

(E.g. see "Anthrotopia: Patterns of Human Habitat" section).

(B) *"Embodiments" or "Personifications"*

Habitatal Habitancy — habitat acting as habitantial agent — *not* habitat affecting habitant...

Habitantial Habitancy — individual Character *in* Personae-roles; roles' actor; the Being behind masks' Becomings...

Habitative Habitancy — patterns of habitation acting as habitantial agent...

Habitudal Habitancy — the form (play) *is* the actor...

(C) *"Behaviors"*

Habitatal Habitation — environment *is* the behavioral action...

Habitantial Habitation — actor *is* the action — *not* merely actor acting...

Habitative Habitation — actions *in* the acting; movings' motives; behavioral subtext in the behaving...

Habitudal Habitation — the form *is* the action...

(D) *"Cultural Forms" or "Modelmaking"*

Habitatal Habitude — environment *is* the form...

Habitantial Habitude — actor *is* the play...

Habitative Habitude — action *is* the form — but *not* its natural or inevitable becoming...

Habitudal Habitude — the art in the art; meaning and purpose in the forms; what is modelled by the making...

The Habitative System, considered in the broadest sense of Place or Locale, obviously includes natural ecologic habitats and manmade architectural habitats, but actually refers to all Context/Constituent interrelationships, whether animate or inanimate, natural or invented. And when factored with the set as habitative modes or operations, then many different kinds and levels of phenomena and worlds can simultaneously participate in these processes:

Habitations of various sorts of energy
At modulated scales of frequency and amplitude
All fit as they inhabit places
Moving in habitable directions
At appropriate rates according to the sequencing of periodic re-inhabitation
And the repatterning of energy-forms in durational relation to other spans.

Although no two habitants can occupy *exactly* the same habitat — selective sensings, attentions and actions may, however, permit habitants to selectively share a general habitat with very different habitations: *tuning* the frequency and amplitude modulations.

> "Though two people may think that they are experiencing the same environment, each individual's environment of the moment is unique and constantly changing. One never really sees, 'see what I mean?' Environment is the result of individual selectivity and response."
> R. Buckminster Fuller, *I Seem To Be a Verb* (1970)

> "Your next-door neighbor...is not a man; he is an environment. He is the barking of a dog; he is the noise of a pianola; he is a dispute about a party wall; he is drains that are worse than yours, or roses that are better than yours." G.K. Chesterton, *The Uses of Diversity* (1920)

This opens the Objective habitats of Natural and Societal Worlds to the Subjective habitats of Individual and Cultural Worlds of meaning. Structural differences and dominances between right and left *habitatal hemispheres* of the brain directly affect perceptual and conceptual habitudes, as do habitats of Freud's conscious/subconscious id, ego, libido, superego, or Jung's extroverted/introverted sensation, thinking, feeling and intuition. As the structure of the subjective internal world engages the structure of the objective external world, they may conjoin in a rich, complex structure of experience — which requires some sort of analogous complexity of *media-form* structuring for the *image-idea* itself to BE an experience of comparable immediacy, intensity, clarity, completeness. Constructing form relationships that model experience inherently objectifies subjective perceptions and intentions while subjectifying a presumed objectivity.

Ultimately, there seem very few types of habitat: habitats of per-mutated spatial patterns—*Pasts' Becomings*—microcosmic worlds as differentially symbolic golden ages and places before and after life; and sacred retreats for spirits shedding difference, joining the flow; or tracery places as continually geologic/geographic "battlefields" of evolution/progression: and habitats of a persistent present—*Being Now*—a magic world where events are omens and image-rites control the events they image; or a proposeful world of constant structural/metaphoric modelmaking giving purpose on out beyond.

VF. (IV./IX.85)

Actor Eli Wallach—during 14 Sept 1975 PBS-TV interview—On the Performer's Death: "I think the way I'd like to go out would be to hear the knock on the dressingroom door—'*PLACES!*'—And I'd be there."

"New York restaurants...caught on that what people really care about is changing their atmosphere for a couple of hours....instead of 'going out to dinner' they'll just be 'going out to atmosphere'....The best atmosphere I can think of is film, because it's three-dimensional physically and two-dimensional emotionally. (pp159–60)

"Your mind makes spaces into spaces. It's a lot of hard work. A lot of hard spaces. As you get older you get more spaces...And more things to put in..." (p143)

"There are different ways for individual people to take over space—to command space. Very shy people don't even want to take up the space that their body actually takes up, whereas very outgoing people want to take up as much space as they can get.

"Before media there used to be a physical limit on how much space one person could take up...People...are the only things that know how to take up more space than the space they're actually in, because with media you can sit back and still let yourself fill up space on records, in the movies, most exclusively on the telephone and least exclusively on television. (p146)

"I like to be the right thing in the wrong space and the wrong thing in the right space....because something funny always happens." (p158)

The Philosophy of Andy Warhol—From A to B & Back Again
(1975, H-B-J, N.Y.)

"Our attention is most easily held hostage when television itself becomes a hostage of terrorists, demonstrators, politicians, and other self-conscious social actors who vie for the chance to become—at least for awhile—our closest neighbor. Paradoxically, TV is both a hijacker and a liberator, hostage and hostage taker. It frees us from the constraints of our isolated physical locations, but flies us to a place that is no place at all."

Joshua Meyrowitz, "The 19-Inch Neighborhood,"
Newsweek (22 July 1985)

IV. WHENCE UPON A HABITATION : Didactic Tongue-Twister

In the energetic blips of Cosmic Habitat—Habitants sprouting, inhabit—and Habitating, spread their Habitudes. Some habits might proliferate to cancel habitation of their habitants, but *reciprocal* habitat-habitant interhabitating may make habitatal form-making habit-forming—and its emanative regenerations habitual.

It is not only how you inhabit the world, but how fully you permit the world to inhabit you in ways that do not inhibit you: in-fluence.

This interhabitation only happens by virtue of building habitat-forms of your own to house worlds that haven't happened yet—but might: con-fluence.

Building these habitat-forms gradually shapes complex experiential belief-constructs inside you: constructive attitudes make healthy habitudes.

And this sighting, insighting, feeling and forming reciprocate as the inhabiting image-idea, which only inheres here in the meaning-content depending how well they cohere as metaphoric media-forms. And they grow and seed only according to how resonantly comprehensive and integral their counterhabitation.

To Habitate is to HAVE—access—which only *seems* like "possession," but can never hold anything, except in exceeding the access by the excessive seeding and giving fresh habitations of mind-in-forms. Habitats must not merely be accessed—especially if their habitants say "No-Trespass"—but must be *constructed* as proposals, though never in forms which interfere with other habitants building their own: grandest stir of metaphors can grow in most modest forms—which may model cosmic worlds!

Wise Habitant's healthfully motivated HABITATION of any Habitat simultaneously shapes purposefully fertile new Habitats by the formings of your constructive Habitudes.

VF. (12.II.85)

V. TOWARD CULTURE OF SOJOURNS

European artists and scientists exiled in the 1930s and '40s "were mostly middle-aged people. Their intellectual suitcases were packed, and they could live anywhere."   Painter William Brice, *Vanity Fair* (Nov 1985)

"I dream of an anchor that could pull the land with it."
                              Stanislaw Lec, *Unkempt Thoughts* (1962)

"The axis of the earth sticks out visibly through the center of each and every town or city."
      "The great thing in this world is not so much where we are, but in what direction we are moving."   Oliver Wendell Holmes (1809–94)

"Individual directions must always be *Toward* (never *Away*) — and TO-WARD is not a PLACE: Places are Loci, Foci, marking Orientation along the way." VF, ix.75 "Aphorisms Toward a Culture of Place from Very Unlikely Places," *WQ*,I:3 (Fall 1975)

But after all, during the short Stewardship of our habitative span, Healthy Places are really WAY-STATIONS: Loci, intersections of events along our way through. So what about places of Origin or Destination? There's a fatality to destiny: an inevitability that even improbable goals die on being achieved and impossible goals are stillborn. But Way-stations can certainly situate origins of experience — coordinate junctures of the base-camp map-and-compass guiding *directions* for how well we move through and *on-from* these known places to the unknowns always out there, where *goals* can never reach (and we can't make the unknowns be the goals, since goals always know their own bounds). "What you depart from is not the way" (Confucian *Chung Yung*, I.2): the way is to be *constantly* working the way *forward*— never for an instant leaving-off working toward clarifying and integrating the most direct and full individual experience to and through some completed forming, without interfering with anyone else doing the same. Might the possibly spiraling growing consequences permit a staying in another way?

For healthy Rites of Passage through different phases of individual development — as through different places or way-stations — directly analogous distinctions must be discerned in Mythic Sojourn.

For meaningful integration and use, four archetypal WAYS or WAYFARINGS need to be distinguished:

(1) the devotional, often processional, homage-tour of *Pilgrimage* to one or a series of foci — acknowledging emulative influence of most perfectly appropriate predecessors;

(2) the testing pursuit of *Quest* — confidence-testing against selfdoubts of comparative achievements: Doubt searches, Confidence pursues, tests;

(3) the discovering journey or voyage of Exploration or *Odyssey* — covering fresh ground on one's own, gathering insights, making connections, returning with revelations; and

(4) the inventive, often transcendent, enterprise of Ad-venture or *Sally* — acting imaginatively unpredictably in proposing visions in forms, the patterns accruing as wisdom — quixotic or daedalian?

Vitality and variety of integral combinations and dominance of combinations always depend on *not* con-fusing the basic distinctions — e.g., the 2nd and 3rd might combine as some sort of Hunting Expedition, and the 3rd and 4th as a Navigational Pathfinding or -making, etc. All Wayfarings involve risk, but the danger is carried along in the baggage of attitudes and skills: and the quality of belief in the trip gives courage or cowardice. Even contemplative retreat may briefly serve as brave pursuit: as method or technique for storing, sorting-through and testing experience, and then deliberately holding-back any impetuses to act on it, such solitude may be prelude to bursts of more intense, articulate, integral and comprehensive imaginative energies in form.

Sitting at edge of the raked-gravel drygardens of Kyoto's Zen Temples in 1954 — and *hearing* the "sea" at Ryoan-ji, and *feeling* the "spray" off the implanted stone "waterfall" and rush of gravel "stream" with the stone "tiger and boat" at Daisen-in — I also carry with me there the deep feeling for the story of Gertrude Stein on her deathbed eight years earlier: "What *is* the answer?" she asks, and when none is forthcoming she laughs, "In that case, what is the question," and then she dies — but it's what she's always been saying. It instantly verifies notions that the questing is usually for answers, but that the Answer *IS* What-is-the-question! Homo Fabre, the Making Mind, just naturally lives with the daily *putting*-of-questions in forms, trusts the uncomfort of putting them. This always disturbs those who are merely asking-for-answers: they seem unable to tolerate reading or viewing all the great works built of questionputting, the very purpose shaped by what they propose—feeling that such works are not quite addressed to Them. "Questions put?—but to whom, and what and whence the answers—or, if all merely rhetorical, then no urgency to attend to them seriously, but since some bestir as hitting close and large, can they be entirely dismissed?" Never seeing that the answer is ONLY in each one continually putting his own largest, deepest questions *in some Form.* So how can a Quest be "Visionary"—since Vision is the insightful beam of eye's mind-light, the aim or Arrow and not the Target. "Thar's Goals (or Grails) in them thar hills" often means disappointment—or depressing letdown and shallow shifting to re-set new goals (and hills) upon attainment. Rather, vectors of directions with endless unanticipated rich *detours,* than tunnelled or funnelled goaling: rigorous programming with flexible means, not fixed end-results. Starting-with or going-after effects produces affectations: starting with conclusions precludes any discovery or invention.

A questing for proofs and truths seems a searching for that which, if and whenever found, would be its death: if Quest seeks its own demise, where is the Vision in that? But the *Quest as test of experience*—the assumptions of experience—is a pursuit with its own rewards of intensifying and extending experience itself: experimenting—starting with trial-and-error—as it rapidly develops to putting and testing hypotheses, builds its fabric of belief. Skeptical (i.e., examining, but *not* doubtful) of accepting others' faiths, Quest's unrelenting pursuit tests experience and builds one's own belief: belief's confident skepticism or faith's doubtful cynicism? *Quest* (supplication as re-quest) is NOT *Pilgrimage*, which can be a constructive work of homage (benediction) for other questions given in works of the predecessors: Horticulturalist Luther Burbank says "I believe in the immortality of influence." Does Searchers' usual confusion of Quest with Pilgrimage have to do with dramatizing the pain, paying homage to the selfsacrifice of their own struggle and search? Picasso says he never searches, he finds and re-finds—and suggests he does so by putting questions in Form. "To search means nothing...To find, is the thing....I paint... what I have found and not what I am looking for....and when a form is realized it is there to live its own life....not made so for transitory purposes, it is to remain what it is and will always have its own form....keep the joy of discovery, the pleasure of the unexpected..." (Picasso, 1923 Statement). Search alone seems selfdoomed—but Quest as test, the Odyssey of discovery, and the Ad-venture of invention open out.

Model aircraft will fly, but they carry no payload and have no destination but the test itself: so, might a more metaphoric *image-modelmaking* pilot its world to point directions marking compass-bearings, such that even if it doesn't quite get there itself, some other pilot will eagerly *persist in building the heading*? A dynamically directional tradition of continually unexpected detours might save us from delusions of "mythmaking" — since Myths cannot be made: they occur as roots, buried deep, of all the crossbred cultural accrual of prior makings. Mindforms — like arrowshafts, even with momentum — without built-in rudderfins and point, have no point: and each Individual Mind's energy-span is not strong or long enough to continually keep working over *techniques* for pulling bowstrings and "metaphysically" aiming with the ultimately pointless! If Art (*ars*) could refer to the inter- and counter-relating insights and image-ideas in proto-typal modelmaking as a *Problem-posing* process, then Craft, Technique or Technology (*technē*) might refer to the articulate fulfilment or completion in appropriate media-forms as a *Problem-solving* process — in an irreversible growing spiral of potential reciprocity. I.e., although no amount of technical processing or craft can ever generate any qualitative leap of invention or new level of idea (only modifications and variations on prior themes), each genuine innovation starts from some individual's experiential problem-posing finding its completion in some appropriate form — and then the experience of that *complete process* may engender a qualitatively deeper and more comprehensive modelling (each slow prior actualization suddenly spawning higher realizations, and not the reverse?).

The more and deeper, the less all lessers matter, and the larger and farther one goes, the smaller he gets — : like the perspective shape of an arrowhead, or a double-vortex?

Pilgrimage's devotions may focus best influences and gather fresh Information — with the rich data of which —

Quest's pursuits may test experience and modify Belief — with the interpretations of which —

Odyssey's explorations may discover connections and reveal Knowledge — with the cognitions of which —

Sally's adventuring proposals-in-form may invent more efficient-complexities and find patterns of Wisdom — with the visions of which, Purposes may be given.

Modern studies of Nature and Society try to give us Information and Knowledge of how to do it, but overlook the Individual's and Cultures' Belief and Wisdom of what is best to do. (See "Worlds and Modes of Meaning" quadrants in "Contextualism & the Habitative Typology" section here). Each work to be worthy must have its arrow built-in: for the arrow of queryputting may point the WAY without itself moving to any answer but the imperative of continually putting the big and deep questions in Form?! And since one takes positions which he moves-on-and-from in relation to others, it's what he *posits* that makes his place: so, the most "sacred places" of all must be to *place-ahead* — to propose as modelmaking, to give purpose in form.

VF. (18.VIII.84 & 18.X.85)

Victor Flach

SACRESCAPES :
Suite of Earthscape Portraits

I. WIND RIVER PERSPECTIVES

Thanks in Memory of Rupert Weeks, Shoshone Storyteller

"Our Land...will last forever....As long as the sun shines and the
waters flow, this land will be here to give life to man and animals....
It was put here for us by the Great Spirit and we cannot sell it because
it does not belong to us....As a present to you, we will give you
anything we have that you can take with you; but the land, never."
Blackfeet Chief, Recorded in a 19th Century Treaty Council

1. IN THE NIGHTCANYON : PRECAMBRIAN CORRIDOR	2. OUT THE DAYCANYON : PRECAMBRIAN ORIFICE
Night sharpens ears & nose	*Day squints eyes & frown*

Who nose
    the rushing
eras, here —
    the sacred
centuries
    breathing down
the Wind River,

fresh sage
and grass,
ancient granite,
water:

Even
    before the
natives, now —
    the savory
cenozoic
    inhalants
exhilerate.

Can eons
    outwait,
can yon
    canyon-face
yawn through
    even demise
of our artifice,

our irrigation,
recreation,
highway and hydro-
electric projects:

That water,
    this wind,
can yawn
    yon rocks
through patient
    eons of
ritual weight.

Wind River Canyon   Indian Lands Wyoming   (Thoreau Journal Quarterly)

II. LOVESCAPE

Dawn
    wakes pineblue
spring-rugged Rockies
    snuggled high
over the smooth-curve
    of warm earthgreen
sage-knoll:

Night
    never tells whether
cool snow-paled
    far-peaks mount
crevice of nearlove,
    of warm earthgreen
knoll-roll.

III. FROM SUMMIT MEADOWS,

When your young stream comes
    to its fall,
its own tragic flush
at the cutrock cliff
makes a filmed spectacle
down the zigged vertical
    then zagged boulderslabs
as your young clear flow

suddenly shows crag white
    in its churned
zigzag cas-
cade to dead-
smooth unroar of hushed
muted rush
    below
your continental divide:

but the waterfall
is no spectacle
    to itself,
nor its own anxious crash
very deeply felt
    by others.

For RE's Teenage Daughter
Fish Creek Falls, Steamboat Spgs

IV. LOVEWATERS

In honor of Priest Sosei,
9th C. Japan, Heian Period

Drink from the sparkling
    ice cool spring
    just below the hidden
        (dung soaked meadow:

Drawn to the rushing
    fresh splash & noise
    of fast passing stream & shore
        (shallows:

Drown in the pull
    of the deep still pool's
    clear mysterious
        (slow roiling surface:

Dream with the stagnant
    swamp pond harboring
    its past, & harvest
)its rich life song.

V. PRAIRIEDEATH

Sun unsets
    dank hillloom in knit
    westbright as it
    highlights hillheights—sil-
        houettes the shade-sliced
        shadowedge of ridgeblade:

Sunken sun
    squeezing bloody light
    from saged skin of
    knollrolls, bleeding hillfolds—
        buries prairie's body by
        west horizon's rise:

Suntil only
    top slit of hilltops lit,
    till bright hilltips, pips,
    loom innate above grave gloom—
        ill loom in eight o'clock light,
        moon-illuminated nine, night, tent.

VI. BUNDLE & CONDUIT : YON LOCAL MISSIVES

1. OUTWARD BOUND BY LOCAL BONDS
Letter to Lamech

We'll be moving soon,
like ancient ocean island-hoppers
        daring horizons —
making *Beyond* their home.

Solutions for packing our cultivations
        all swimmingly
coming with genetic encodings
        and microchip memories,

        and we're tuning-up
fuels and ships to ride, like they,
        the winds and currents —
always knowing just where they were.

But before the crafting outward
        needs its starmaps to
navigate the mostly knowns,
        some cartographers of

        imagination visioning outward
propose clear worlds of reciprocity
        by analogous structures —
the main cultivations to be carried.

Can't — this trip — really leave the old
        neighborhood till we can
cart the whole garden and all seasons
        of regenerative embodied mind.

2.X.83

2. BEYOND'S REJOINDER
Laertes' Reply

Beyond the horizon!
but it's always receding as you approach:
　　...know how curiosity
goads your venture to journey, explore,
　　discover and order
for your own going—and bet you
　　can get there, but *what for,*
without rounding returns in forms
　　for your own growing?

　　Can sailing-out for possible
beaches ever really arrive,
　　when only richly formed
re-arrivals can also carry the journey:
　　Can the carrying-forth
internourish without coming-back with the
　　finds of your combing—
or do acts and accidents without feedback
　　only speak to those winds?

　　Does going-out need
bringing-back to feed the cultivations—
　　not merely for what starfaring
means to how the tribe fares, but how you
　　re-seed your own receding:
What point is "Beyond" without the rejoinder?
　　Ah! your own return's no concern
since the log's message comes on light's
　　passage (we'll miss you).

6.1.84

VICTOR FLACH

Lowry Burgess

The Quiet Axis

The Quiet Axis is an aesthetic structure that opens a benevolent revelation that extends through the earth stretching out in the the cosmos from the far side of the moon to the Large Cloud of Magellan. There are seven zones or aspects of its manifestation beginning with the Inclined Galactic Light Pond in Bamiyan, Afghanistan (1968-1974) passing through the earth to the second work called The Utopic Vessel (1974-1979) in the South Pacific Ocean beside Easter Island and from there extending into outer space and the southern heavens to the third realization called The Gate into Aether (1979-1988) and then returning through the earth and backward in time to the fourth twinned work called The Boundless Cubic Aperture (1980-1995). The fifth work Memory and Forms of the Unmanifest touches The Boundless Cubic Aperture on the far lunar surface. The sixth and seventh aspects address the center of the earth and the violet stellar source that is centered in the Large Cloud of Magellan, a source 50,000 times more bright and energetic than the sun.

The first three aspects are summarily described herein. The fourth, The boundless Cubic Lunar Aperture is somewhat more described in the text that follows the summary statements.

I. The Inclined Galactic Light Pond
Bamiyan, Afghanistan 1968-1974

The Inclined Galactic Light Pond consists of twelve holographic plates of waterlilies and stars buried in six pits in the earth along a mile and one-half axis oriented to magnetic north/south. Each plate is buried at an angle of our galaxy at sunrise for each of the twelve months, thereby indicating fragments of the surface of a lake with waterlilies which was placed in the plane of the Milky Way Galaxy at sunrise. The stars on each plate indicate a vertical shaft of stellar space beneath and above the earth at midnight for each month. The

Inclined Galactic Light Pond thereby creates a new virtual center for the Earth.

II. The Utopic Vessel
South Pacific Ocean, Rapa Nui (Easter Island) 1974-1979

The Utopic Vessel is a crystal spherical vessel 24 inches in diameter placed on the bottom of the Pacific Ocean near Easter Island exactly opposite, through the center of the earth, from the Inclined Galactic Light Pond in Bamiyan, Afghanistan. The vessel contains an open holographic glass book in which each page is a 20 foot shaft of open space lying open in a nest of pollen, saffron, and yeast sealed in a honey filled container. The inner vessel rests on a solid copper heptagonal form which in turn sits in a sea of pure vermilion containing pulverized holograms of peachlike forms. All of this rests in the outer container which is inscribed with all the visible stars of the southern heavens.

III. The Gate Into Aether, Wreath of Sounding
Outer Space Above Rapa Nui 1976-1988

The Gate Into Aether is a torus form 18 inches in diameter consisting of 18 sections of frozen water taken from the mouths of 18 great rivers throughout the world (Nile, Tigris-Euphrates, Indus, Ganges, Yang Tzu, Congo, Mississippi, Colorado, Rio Grande, St. Lawrence, Amazon, Yukon, Danube, Rhine, etc.). These waters are each combined with one other special water source, i.e., lake, geyser, glacier, well, waterfall, etc. Between the 18 frozen sections of water are sonic holograms of wave fronts of sound of the ecstatic singing of peoples and animals on the surface of 40 million year old petrified leaves. In outer space, above The Utopic Vessel, this form will sublime as minute crystals of ice some of which will be carried into space and others return to the earth as a minute rain.

IV. The Boundless Cubic Lunar Aperture

The Boundless Cubic Lunar Aperture is a hypercubic form or set of nested cubes extending in a 19 billion year time frame. At its center is a cubic vaccuum surrounded on six faces by holographic images of nothing. This central cubic form floats in a shadowy glass cube containing all the elements of the periodic table, gaseous, liquid and solid combined with a distillation (retrieved from the surface of the Dead Sea) of waters taken from 18 great rivers and 18 other sources gathered from all over the earth. On the top and bottom of this cubic chamber are two holographic texts which in the direct light of outer space will radiate into the space above and below this cubic heart. This is the part of the Boundless Cubic Lunar Aperture that is to be taken into outer space by the NASA Shuttle and in space released to tumble weightless and to proclaim its message of release and reassurance. Subsequently, it is to be brought back to earth where the cubic container becomes the sappy center of a 40 million year old petrified sycamore which in turn hovers within an outer chamber that generates a permanent magnetic field. This outer chamber is made of alternating layers of blue pearl granite and bronze. Its top and bottom are holographic plates of extreme depth indicating a view though the Quiet Axis. This cubic form is, in turn embedded in the 400 million year old residue of a lake which is now beside Sandy Pond in Lincoln, Massachusetts.

Slowly, the Boundless Cubic Lunar Aperture unfolds and gathers a dark and metamorphic furnace resulting from the shock of the Utopic Vessel's encounter with the earth beneath the Pacific Ocean near Easter Island. That passionate shock is carried through the earth gathering form and substance in its descent through earthly material time. The result of plunging downward through the layers of the earth's crust is folding time backward, falling through earth matter but also through earth time emerging in the layers of rock created four hundred million years ago which is the alluvial remnants of a lake then in the vicinity of northern Afghanistan, now beside Sandy Pond near Walden pond. Its residual energy twists and cracks its heart, The Boundless Aperture, loose and it is thrown, falls into space by a human fulfillment of an ancient geological upthrust, an earth wave breaking open downward and backward in time/space.

As the Boundless Cubic Lunar Aperture falls, it gathers to itself two branching transformations caused by the sublime burning of the Gate Into Aether. The leaves of ecstatic sound tumble backward burning, falling through the earth joining leaf to twig, twig to branch, and branch to trunk forming the double grown black crystal tree of darkness which emerges in the bottom of the Grand Canyon in the emerald Havasu pool and it is retrieved there. Equally, the sublimed crystals of water from the Gate Into Aether reenter the atmosphere and pass through the earth to emerge as a pure and unified droplet on the surface of the Dead Sea, summoned by the words:

Bring forth the waters of this world,
And let it surround these people,

For they bring that which is one to the earth:
And bind the energies to make it gyrate and soften
Let it bring comfort, clarity, and solace
To everything contained within this world.

This purified water was distilled and retrieved from the surface of the Dead Sea and brought up to become the central sap within the dark petrified tree. The dark tree and the pure water are indrawn to the Boundless Cubic Lunar Aperture by its magnetic vacuous force as it falls downward in time and space where they all join beside Sandy Pond.

From there it continues its backward temporal fall, it still passes outward along the lunar eclipse shadow to the oldest rock layers of the far side of the moon into the crater Korolev where it engenders and binds its hysteron proteron, its unseen lunar twin resting beneath material time in the solar system. This is the Quiet Axis' pedestal; font, and aperture into the void:

Desolate source,
Neither object nor belief,
Tree of winged flesh convulsed
Bear us still, still bears us.

The essence of The Boundless Cubic Lunar Aperture is the awe of confrontation with utter otherness. The otherness of vast neutrality in which the pressure of the unmanifest is felt against a fundament of nonbeing. Between the unmanifest and nonbeing consciousness is ground to dust. Such enormous and symmetrical weights inexorably condemn every effort.

The Boundless Cubic Lunar Aperture is the vortex of this dust falling in darkness beyond all darkness, in the dim glow that is neither light nor heat but the thousandfold twilight of intuition. A territory where matter and emotion are indivisible in darkness, in an autumnal fall of burnt shadows. It becomes the well, the destination, the shepherd, the place wherein burnt rivers meet.

The Boundless Cubic Lunar Aperture is stubbornly and obsessively concentrated upon this darkest void of oblivion, the death inside death, beyond forsakeness which opens and is framed in its unswerving gaze. It does not turn back but presses onward into a crushing nonpresence, the abiding of absolute absence.

There a lifting, persistent, eternal form is felt as a grounding far beyond even faith or hope. That upholdingness sustains the mercy of poetic intuition which draws everything lost or futile to itself with great calm and sure carrying care. We have begun to see with our Eyes, to hear with our Ears, and to touch with our Hands, a placement that wraps us round more surely than the bonds of gravity, for through great desire, from the enormity of endlessness, each to each is drawn, and stands inside out, a wildly burning fleshlike tree of wings, branch to root connected, shedding sparks of laughter, touching exactly this, this, this, speaking:

> Peace comes as you bring it.
> All in being is what you make it.
> There is no becoming no goal.
> The right way is wrong and the wrong way is right.
> What is done is done.
> What is faced
> Without beginning or end.
> Time is the difference between the inner and the outer.
> A form of linear thought caught within existence
> Linked with the physical as gravity.
> With time energy picks up form,
> Without time energy changes dimension.
> We come into an expession of the Eternal.
> The physical world is for the ripening and healing of the
> Eternal.
> Everything is formed in the image of the Eternal,
> Reaching through turning inside out.
> Therefore, nature and its all contains the links to the Eternal.
> The many energies and links are like a fabric, all one,
> But separate strands, each with its own knowledge and purpose,
> Equally important, a flowing mesh without gaps.
> The balancing of all these energies is the greatest form of love.
> And through truth the creative world is linked to that Eternal
> The clearest insight into truth is through joy.
> The pure waters of the earth come from the Eternal.
> Therefore be one with the earth as one would make the sand
> fire,
> And the fire sun.

Interview with Lowry Burgess

conducted by Thomas Frick

LB: This work began in '68. Basically my activities were more fragmented in structure before. I was doing huge paintings and at the same time a lot of environmental work with domes, and building structures for teachers and children. I was building a lot of stuff outdoors and involved in urban activities and alternative education in the 60's. And I was fairly active in protest actions against the war; so that brought a lot of pressure on the art-making to re-define itself in relationship to the world. What happened was that the war was getting worse in '68 and I was very depressed one evening, and went out on my porch after the evening news, having done quite a few things, and . . . sort of asking myself what one could do to put weight on the other side of the fence and I had a vision, if you want, of a lake sloping in the air in twilight . . . I think it was in the autumn of '68. And I saw this lake sloping in the air in Afghanistan with water-lilies blooming on its surface, very clearly. It was like—okay, you want to put something on the other side? You go to the lake in air in the middle of Asia!

So the next six years of my work were sort of consumed on the edges of how I could approach such a task. A whole lot of bumps and terrors along the way, but I found the medium that I needed in holography, and I found the context when several things fell through on another project. I got very sick; finally it was utterly clear that if I didn't go off and do this thing I'd have some real problems! So I packed up my family and went off to Afghanistan, and did the work.

When we were there it was very clear, in the process of doing the work, that the larger thing wasn't finished. Because all the time I was in Bamiyan I had the sense of tremendous warmth and rich color, particularly vermilion, in the form of copper, coming up from the ground beneath me. So there was something else emerging! On the other side of the world!

It took me the next four years to formulate the work called Utopic Vessel, which in every way is a reversal of the material in the Afghan work. The Afghan work is very dark and somber, very like a requiem in structure.

TF: How did the Afghan people receive the work you did there?
LB: They received it very well, much better than my friends and people here! But insofar as it's an Islamic culture, it's not an untoward thing to go a great distance based on a quest and a vision. Those kinds of things are very much a part of the culture. People live to do their hejira and to go to Mecca. What I was doing was not unusual beyond my being an American. What's nice is that now there's a story in the valley, of the lake that's not there. After we left, people coming through were told about this invisible lake.

It took the next four years to get to the work in the Pacific Ocean, the Utopic Vessel. It's a tremendously brilliant, tense, compacted work, compared to the expansive darkness of Afghanistan. And again, in the process of my preparing all of it and getting there and doing the actual labor, it was clear that—aha!—it's not done yet! There's more and more! And it's been happening ever since. As I climb the rungs of this peculiar ladder it seems that there are always more rungs above it and beneath it. So the whole thing keeps branching out above and below me; as I climb I'm able to see new parts of the whole, but it's not something I know ahead of time; it's very inductive.

TF: So the Utopic Vessel is on the opposite side, precisely . . .
LB: Yeah, on the opposite side of the world, exactly opposite Afghanistan, in the bottom of the Pacific Ocean, near Easter Island. It was fabricated and put together in a ceremonial way on the edge of a very large volcano. . . . Then the third work emerged from—I don't know if you know Edgerton's photo of a drop of milk—
TF: Oh the strobe flash thing—I have a postcard of it.
LB: Yeah. Almost all of the next set of things come from hydrodynamics. When you drop a drop of milk this crown of little droplets arises around the edge of the splash. Well, it's as if by dropping the Utopic Vessel I set the reciprocal motion. The third and fourth works are each reciprocal motions, to each other, and precisely from that vessel being dropped.

The fourth work is going down, while the third work is going up! Imagine the waters of the world being lifted, 18 droplets, or 18 sources. What I did was to go and collect water from the mouths of 18 big rivers, all over the world, and then I collected 18 other sources, or *conditions* of water, very special conditions — ponds, pools, geysers, glaciers, or whatever, very old. 36 waters in all, very old and powerful, contained in this ring of ice. Which is an elaborate set of forms derived from geometries taken out of the golden section. In the interface of those pieces of water are very thin slices of petrified wood, a tree I brought up from the bottom of the Grand Canyon — which is an elaborate story. On the surfaces of all these slices of petrified wood are sonic holograms, sounds of animals, creatures, plants, all over the world. The characteristic of their sound is ecstasy . . .

TF: How is this done?

LB: It's a picture of a wavefront of sound in space. It's as if you're photographing sound waves as they're coming towards a surface.

TF: How is that applied to the stone?

LB: It's a holographic process, like sound waves being revealed as sight; it would look like a wavy set of patterns in space upon surfaces of these thin, very leafy pieces of very old wood. That work means to be taken into space and placed over the top of the Pacific work, and, when it's up there, to dissolve the ice that's supplying these crystals; these then tumble and burn up . . .

TF: It would be jettisoned from the space shuttle itself?

LB: Yeah, and then dissolve. What's interesting is that I approached NASA to fly this, and they want to fly it, but they want to fly it later. They asked me if there wasn't another work that I wanted to fly first, and I said yes — the internal part of the fourth work. I described that and they said, Oh yes, let's fly that first, and then we'll fly the third work later.

TF: What was the reasoning behind that?

LB: The third work requires too many exceptions to their rules, and they didn't want that to happen right off. See, I would be their first art project and if I broke too many of the rules then . . . it would be hard to control the situation, in terms of what they're doing.

The fourth work is the dropping *through* the Earth and backwards into time of, as if the Utopic Vessel continued to pass through the Earth. It's moving through matter and moving backwards through time. It's becoming very old and very substantial, and changing all its geometry as it shifts from droplet to cube, as it becomes a kind of hypercube. And it emerges on the other side of the Earth. The center of the work is a cubic vacuum chamber; it's as if that vacuum is calling to itself, gathering these things together as part of the axis . . .

TF: So what part of this will they launch?

LB: The very center, the cubic vacuum chamber, which is floating, and surrounded by 6 holograms of nothing—another long story!

TF: The ultimate focus. . . .

LB: Which floats in the distilled waters—the 36 waters that I distilled on the surface of the Dead Sea. So the waters have come back through the Earth, and emerged as a purified droplet, above the surface of the Dead Sea. That droplet is being retrieved, okay? The leaves have burned up and fallen backwards through time and re-emerged in the Grand Canyon, as a petrified log which I retrieved from the bottom of the Grand Canyon. So there are two-billion-year old layers of rock.

These are kind of like Paul Bunyan, reaching *down* into the Earth to retrieve fragments of the already disappearing third work—bringing them together into this focal point, which is the Boundless Aperture. This little cube then floats inside another cube, which has all the waters of the world distilled in it. And the inside that is the whole periodic table. So I have all the elements of the Earth—trace elements, everything. It'll be in that water, in that chamber, and that'll be sealed. It's like a model of all the elements of creation.

TF: Actual samples of the elements?

LB: Yeah. And in such a way that the whole work is a ten-billion-year process. Natural chemistry will take ten billion years to stabilize it.

TF: So it's like this huge sort of time organism as well as space, turning in and on itself. . . .

LB: Literally, this work is pursuing the bottom of material time in our part of the universe. In which ultimately part of itself breaks loose and goes to the far side of the Moon, which is where the oldest rocks are. So ultimately it pops out underneath the Moon. It's like this prophecy that goes down to declare itself beneath our time or our material presence.

TF: I can't help but think of the slab in *2001*.

LB: Yeah, yeah. It is strange that I'm winding up in a similar kind of spot, but it goes down there to declare a very different contract—and sort of corrects the commas in the initial contract.

TF: Anti-alien in comparison with the slab . . .

LB: All my work is very anti-science-fiction. I have nothing to do with that sort of thing. It's aimed at our view of ourselves, and the Earth, and belonging in the universe, and getting up there, and out, and back, with the imagination. So you could think of The Quiet Axis as a ladder or a tree that the imagination can climb out and get back on, and establish a very different perception.

The work that NASA's going to fly will be the very center of this cube, which then comes back here to this slab of very old geology, the oldest stuff around here, an ancient lake bed. Inside this massive pile of rock, the cube will be seized inside the petrified tree which hovers in a permanent magnetic field. So the cube that has gone into space, has floated up there, becomes weightless, declared itself, comes back to the Earth, and brings back that kind of weightlessness, and becomes a permanently hovering thing, sort of pulling or tugging at the Earth to remind itself of this kind of free spirit. So it's a very strange kind of judo! My own sort of peculiar form of judo! Something having been weightless and free, having chirped and squawked, comes back, goes back inside the Earth in a very complex way and pulls at it constantly.

TF: All of these ideas touch certainly on metaphysical and religious ideas about what art is, sacred concerns, what we are and what the planet is and what space is. You have to go back to primitive civilizations building huge monuments, orienting things in cosmic space, to find anything comparable. What's in between us and them?

LB: I think that contemporary Vedic culture is involved in vast cosmic structures. Some of their things are *awfully* close to things that I've been trying to do. They, and I think also shamanic cultures in the Siberian north, have aspects of a lot of what I've been doing.

TF: What kinds of things?

LB: The notion of cosmic structure and the invocation of larger relationships — art to society, art to both the individual and the universe. The notion of involving the individual in a sort of micro/macro unity. Art becomes a structure, a ceremony, process or whatever you want to call it, a communal and in our case *planetary* being. There are people all over the world giving this kind of structure to their particular societies. And it's not a well-known story. It's not particularly marketable.

TF: Certainly as far as the Western world view, or lack of it, goes it's a more desperate kind of event because we're rapidly destroying any sense of. . . .

LB: A lot of it has to do with a revelation of the Earth as garden. Sort of delivering the vision that Socrates had in that last speech, of a kind of paradise that wraps around, an interpenetrating paradise, with that NASA view of the globe which he had. He saw it utterly like he was describing a NASA photo. At the same time he saw that the Earth we see in a NASA photo was wrapped in a glorious perfection; he gave us an intimation of that. It's very believable. It's in the *Phaedo*, the last speech, if you read that it's just stunning. He describes the Earth as self-sustaining in space, and he goes on to describe the Mediterranean as basically small, because there are many other such places on the Earth. And as water was to air, so air was to the aether. So if we could peek our consciousness above the air and into the aether, we would see as much more clearly as those who peek from the water into the air.

TF: It too is a kind of ladder.

LB: An *amazing* piece of stuff, so untypically unSocratic — "Look, there's no debate about this, these are my last words! This is the way it is! We're not *discussing* this!" But I believe it. I don't think Plato distorted very much. You hear a very authentic voice, even in translation.

TF: How about the actual manufacturing of the stuff that you do?

LB: Holograms get made in England. I work with all kinds of people — holographers, chemists. Everett Turner of Amherst put all the elements together for me.

TF: It's an amazing high-tech process going immediately into a spiritual condition. . . .

LB: On a funny level it's very ancient and very new.

TF: Have you got the transfer of this thing to the Moon worked out?

LB: That I *hope* will be my third work with them. I want to fly this work, then I want to fly the ice work, then I want to do the Moon work. We're going back to the 'nineties. I'm planning a very strange thing for the other side of the Moon — barely there! Barely an objective presence . . . but a strong *subjective* presence!

Douglas Spangle

Tibetan New Year's in Portland

In red rage,
the Red Sultan bore down upon me,
> swinging like a bolo the holy censer edged with
> razorblades;
> death warrants, search warrants and false
> confessions
> spilling from his hashmarked sleeves like hidden
> cards;
and I said this is not real
> but in the imagination only.

White with rage,
the asylum attendant seized me,
> smelling of Lysol, face puffed and white as
> Wonderbread,
> a sickly easter lily stuck behind one ear,
> a syringe full of morphine peeping from his
> shirt pocket;
and I said this is not real
> but in the imagination only.

In black rage,
the black bellman clattered after me,
> ragged robe flapping, flaying the air like a
> crow's wing;
> purple buboes like purses bulging from his
> armpits,
> a spaniel-sized rat, ember-eyed, on a leash;
and I said this is not real
> but in the imagination only.

The green generalissimo, raging
Grendel, saber rattler, grabbed me
                    by the shoulder, spun me around, mor-
                        tared a full round
                    of martial law at me, promised death on a
                        dunghill
                    at Vladivostok, a ticket on Yagoda's train;
and I said this is not real
                    but in the imagination only.

In a rage, the yellow-fevered
stubbleface lurched out of an alley at me,
                stinking of futility, his pockets full of onces and
                    wases,
                an empty winebottle and a half-eaten can of vienna
                    sausages,
                drunk as a lord on his own hopelessness;
and I said this is not real
                    but in the imagination only.

Blue in the face with rage, the pinstriped
financier lunged at me
                with a tickertape sickle and a hatchetman mask,
                a fistful of frozen assets, signing the Golgotha payroll,
                consigning Welfare scum to petroleum tarpits;
and I said this is not real
                    but in the imagination only.

None of you are real, I said.
                        Deputies of darkness,
                        painted puppets on a lacquered
                            screen,
none of you are real.
                        I'll shout my heathen voice
                        through your imaginary fabric;

                        this is not the true night.
                        Where is the true night?

And the grayvoiced fog
slunk after me,

          pervading the air like neurosis,
          everywhere around me.
          And the gray fog was the worst;
it was real
       and a dream,
       a screen
       for the imagination.

Contributors' Notes

José Argüelles is Director of Communications for the Planet Art Network. He has also published many books, among them *Mandala*, and *Earth Ascending*.

Sven Birkerts is currently completing *Hamann's Bone: Essays in the Language of Poetry*.

David Boardman is a native of Bend, Oregon, and has sung basso with the Portland Symphonic Choir in performances of Orff's *Carmina Burana* and Handel's *Messiah*.

David Brennan is a publisher and poet in the grand tradition.

Lowry Burgess first appeared in North Atlantic books ten years ago, doing the cover for Richard Grossinger's *The Provinces*. He heads the graduate program and teaches at Massachusetts College of Art.

Grady Clay is a consulting editor specializing in the urbanizing environment. From 1960 to 1984 he edited the international journal *Landscape Architecture*. His books include *Close-Up: How to Read the American City*, and *Alleys, A Hidden Resource*.

Jesseca Ferguson is a visual artist (and francophone/francophile) living and working in Boston.

Victor Flach has completed four multiwalled murals in public buildings, including the two-wall, three-storey "Northwest Spiral" in the University of Wyoming Science Center; he teaches painting; design, visual theory, structure and metaphor; and iconography at the University of Wyoming in Laramie.

Thomas Frick is an art critic living in Boston.

Jean Genet's novels and plays are among the most celebrated works of the twentieth century.

Richard Grossinger is an anthropologist and writer, the author of three recent books, *Planet Medicine*, *The Night Sky*, and *Embryogenesis*. He is the publisher of North Atlantic Books.

Lars Gustafsson has published in virtually every area of *belles lettres:* novels, stories, poems, essays, drama, criticism, and journalism. His novels are published in the United States by New Directions.

Friedrich Hölderlin, born in 1770, was one of the greatest of German poets. The last thirty-six years of his life were spent in an almost total poetic silence.

Mikhail Horowitz is renowned as a stand-up comedian in the New York area. He is also an artist and poet and works for a newspaper in Kingston. His book *Big League Poets* was published by City Lights, and his colored baseball cards and poems appear in two North Atlantic baseball anthologies, *The Temple of Baseball* and *Baseball I Gave You All the Best Years of My Life.*

Susan Howe is the author of seven books of poems, the most recent being *Pythagorean Silence* and *Defenestration of Prague*. Her book *My Emily Dickinson* was published by North Atlantic Books in the Fall of 1985.

Bettina Knapp is Professor of Romance Languages at Hunter College; also Lecturer at the Jung Foundation of New York. She has published critical studies on many twentieth-century literary figures. Among her most recent books are *Archetype, Dance, and the Writer* and *A Jungian Approach to Literature.*

Richard LeMon lived for three years in Asia, two in Japan and one in the People's Republic of China. He has studied the *I Ching* since 1974 and has written a book about it.

David Lloyd has lived and been schooled in Belfast and Cambridge, and spent several years in Antwerp. He teaches at Berkeley and is finishing a book on Irish nationalism and poetics, translation and parody.

Henri Michaux wrote many books of poetry, and experimental prose. His texts recounting his experiences with mescaline and hashish are small classics. He was also well known as an artist. He died in 1985.

Mit Mitropoulos divides his time between the MIT Center for Advanced Visual Studies and the deserted waterline realm here written about.

Howard Norman is a recipient of the first Whiting Foundation Writing Awards. His translations and tellings of Indian tales are well known. His first novel, *Northern Lights* will appear in 1986.

Novalis (Friedrich Philipp von Hardenberg 1772-1801) was a mystical Christian who has come to represent the movement known as German Romanticism.

Thomas Paladino edited the now defunct *Third Wind*, a journal of poetry and myth. The first two volumes of his sequential long poem "Presences" were published last year by the Charles River Press.

Richard Sieburth teaches French and comparative literature at New York University.

Phil Sittnick lives on the coast of Massachusetts that is the locus for his poems here. Other poems of his have been published in *Truck* and *Aux Arcs*.

Alex Shoumatoff is a staff writer for *The New Yorker*. Among his books are *Florida Ramble, Russian Blood*, and the recent *The Mountain of Names*.

Douglas Spangle co-hosts an open-mike poetry night in Portland, Oregon. He has recent work in *The Third Wind, Soundings East*, and *Hub Bub*.

George Steiner is Extraordinary Fellow of Churchill College, Cambridge and Professor of English at the University of Geneva. Two of his recent books are *Antigones* and *Martin Heidegger*.

Georg Trakl and Rilke were beneficiaries of Ludwig Wittgenstein's anonymous disbursement of his patrimony. Rilke asked rhetorically of Trakl, "Who may he have been?" Trakl died at the age of 26 of a cocaine overdose.

Robin E. van Löben Sels was born and raised in California but now lives in New York and Connecticut, earning a living as a Jungian psychoanalyst, and also writing.

Edwin Wilmsen is Professor of Anthropology in the African Studies Center of Boston University. He recently published *Killer Chill: Poems for the South African Peoples' Struggle*. He travels.

Geoffrey Young edits THE FIGURES publications in Great Barrington, Massachusetts, and, as a poet, is author of numerous books, including *Subject to Fits*.

Barbara Martz *in memoriam.*